Dishonourable DISCHARGE

Yarns of Wine, Women and Waves

'MY CABIN'S FULL OF HOOKERS
AND THE CAPTAINS ON HIS ROUNDS'

ROBIN TICKNER

Published by New Generation Publishing in 2013

Copyright © Robin Tickner 2013

First Edition

The author asserts the moral right under the Copyright, Designs and Patents Act 1988 to be identified as the author of this work.

All Rights reserved. No part of this publication may be reproduced, stored in a retrieval system or transmitted, in any form or by any means without the prior consent of the author, nor be otherwise circulated in any form of binding or cover other than that which it is published and without a similar condition being imposed on the subsequent purchaser.

www.newgeneration-publishing.com

New Generation Publishing

Dedicated to my family Mum and Dad and their offspring's, Jeremy, Joff, Buster, and best mates Richard Oxley, Alan Jones and the unforgettable Big Dave. A bad sail with these guys was always better than a good day in the office!

I would also like to raise a glass to those privileged passengers who were lucky enough to sail on the beautiful lavender hulled Union Castle ships between Southampton and South Africa back in the halcyon days of sea travel. This book will raise a wry smile at the antics of the officers in their efforts to entertain their charges and really what went on up on the bridge and way down below in the bowels of the ships as we endeavoured to keep to the companies tight sailing schedule.

Perhaps some salty sons of the sea who ran Union Castle passenger ships and Clan Line cargo ships may recognise some of the stories and recall how much fun it was to be young and carefree tramping around the globe visiting ports as yet spared from hordes of package holidaymakers.

Slightly closer to shore there are hundreds of hardy sailors who at an early age were cajoled into tiny sailing dinghies on numerous rivers and lakes to learn the skills of sailing with its utterly confusing vocabulary and the additional benefit of a quick dunking if or when you got it wrong. The sensible ones got married and took up gardening otherwise you graduated to offshore racing which involved hours if not days crashing about the North Sea. All this in a variety of sailing craft ranging from really wet and uncomfortable so called classics to state of the art flyers. As any cash strapped skipper will tell you the two best times for a boat owner are the day you buy a yacht and the day you sell her!

If you drank warm Watneys Red Barrel, wore flares, Chelsea boots and a Ben Sherman shirt, rode a Royal Enfield motor bike or Lambretta scooter, knew all the Beatles or Stones lyrics and struggled to buy a condom you may find some resonance in the meandering stories of the boy who ran away to sea, twice.

Contents

Casting Off	5
College Days	12
Surfing Dudes	22
Zulu Wars	26
Mombasa	39
The 'Chippies' Story	49
An Engineers Tale	51
Homeward Bound	69
Early Days	73
Back to work	103
Passenger Ship Day's	114
Banned off Deck	150
An Officer and a Gentleman	154
Clan Boats	170
Tying the Knot	181
Swallowing the anchor	189
Speed to meet your Need	191
The Bosch Years	201
The Navigators Story	207
Arse in a sling	218
Scramble	223
Decline and fall	228
UKOBA	232
Jeep Drivers Bum	236
Fly Détente and Die happy	243
The Buckley Goblets	248
11 Chapel Rd	257
I Get around	259
Making Fast	263
Finished with Engines	265

Casting Off

Don't you just love the flamboyant language of theatre reviewers?

If this was a play the critics would hopefully say 'a rollicking ride through the authors misspent youth, bawdy tales of exotic countries, eccentric characters and rib cracking mishaps served up with a heady mix of wine, woman and waves. It had me rolling in the aisles'

Well it's not a play, I'm not sure if it's even a book, more a jumble of memories! Just recently a well read, bordering on sophisticated friend, enquired what genre my scribbling's fell into. Well for a start I wouldn't know a genre if it stood up and bit me on the arse. I'm just a simple sailor with a fondness for the occasional libation who's had the luck to share some special times with odd members of the opposite sex and I do mean odd! For a quick insight into what I mean check out page 41 for the Great Mombassa Brothel story.

So how did I end up at sea? There certainly wasn't a Tickner seafaring tradition. Grandad galloped around the Somme on a horse pulling a field gun, and Dad had been a Major in the Indian Army, doing things with tanks in the late thirties and early forties or the last unpleasantness with our German friends as Mother would have it.

Father did build a kit boat in the garden when I was about two, called a Foil. It was eight foot long; Dad was six foot tall, so not much room for the rest of the family. Anyway it got nicked the day after it was launched. I suspect that mother, suitably traumatised by the maiden voyage, under cover of night, pushed it out to sea. Undeterred father built another dinghy named impressively the 'Yachting World Pram', in which he taught my three brothers and I how to sail.

Father used the same teaching system he had

perfected on land educating his sons to ride bikes. First select a suitably steep hill, preferably with a major road crossing at the bottom to add the additional fear factor. Place quaking child on saddle, push off heartily and by the time you hit the crossing, well lo and behold, you could ride! A word of caution here roads were much quieter then. As a finale to the whole exercise, mother usually had a heavily soiled item of underwear to include in the Monday wash!

The nautical version of this rather extreme training method involved similar principles. The vessel, with child strapped securely on board was launched firmly away from the beach preferably with an offshore gale blowing. Hopefully before crossing the shipping lanes the child had learnt to sail.

It is no wonder my kid brother Buster, in later years, joined the RNLI to compensate for father's rather cavalier approach to sail training.

I began this exposé of 'the life and times of a sailor' whilst taking part in the 1999 Atlantic Rally for Cruising Yachts sailing the trade winds from the Canaries to St. Lucia in the Caribbean. I was on a Bavaria 35, which is a type of boat, not a middle aged German gay, just in case you were making an early judgement on my sexual preferences. Unfortunately the trade winds did not cooperate, twenty three days to cross the pond! Vikings rowed it more quickly, so I had ample time to pen this script.

The call of the sea came down from my eldest brother Jeremy's choice of career, because, in my parent's opinion as the first offspring, he could obviously walk on water. Even now the mention of his name invokes a reverential bow in the direction of Mecca.

Jeremy ran away to sea after serving a marine apprenticeship with the British and Commonwealth

Shipping Company. Oldies amongst you might remember them for their fleet of lavender hulled Union Castle passenger ships. He appeared spasmodically throughout my school years bearing gifts from far off lands, mainly sandalwood elephants, telling stories which usually made Mother leave the room.

After several abortive sessions with the school career officer, I was running out of ideas for my future. How in hell at the tender age of fifteen are you supposed to know what you are going to do for the next fifty years?

Sitting here at my chart table with five hundred miles of the Atlantic between Wizzo, my sail boat, and Gibraltar having just turned fifty, I still do not have an answer for that one.

However, after listening to a particularly lurid tale from Jeremy involving a nubile woman and a coconut, my mind was made up, a sailor I would be. That was the easy bit, but what type of sailor? An engineer, a deck officer, a sparky or perhaps a purser, and how did one join?

In 1968 the British economy had tightened up, jobs were harder to find and qualifications were vital. With the help of Dad and on the back of Jeremy's reputation, I managed to bluff my way into an engineering apprenticeship with the B&C shipping company, provided I passed several GCE's and an entrance exam.

To sit this exam I was sent to the Warsash School of Seamanship situated on the banks of the river Hamble in Hampshire for a three day induction course.

On the first afternoon whilst taking a stroll through the schools extensive grounds, I met a bloke dressed in a long black boat cloak sitting miserably in a rowing boat at the end of a pier. His task apparently was to greet any royalty who might happen by. Asking the obvious question, it appears that at no time in the school's history, had Liz Windsor or indeed any of her family graced the schools pontoon. This was hardly surprising as 'sod all' ever happens in Warsash.

I was sharing a bunkroom with four other students, one of whom, can you believe this, was under a months discipline with no shore leave. His crime was carving his girlfriends initials on a window ledge! As I lay in bed that night I considered whether this was the seat of learning I could aspire to in my pursuit of a life at sea.

I thought of the poor sod in the rowing boat, the Dickensian discipline, but worst of all, and to my mind the greatest cardinal sin in the world was I had discovered the school had no bar! What did these guys do for fun? As in how did Oliver Reed celebrate?

After a fitful night's sleep I was rudely awaken at six by a large bright light stuck in my face, closely followed by a glass eye. An invitation to run around the grounds was offered by the owner of the optical aid, who turned out to be an extremely fit bald-headed individual. He was wearing a faded tracksuit covered with badges denoting years of marathon achievements. Now I don't do marathons, so after duly considering his suggestion, and taking into account the previous night's thoughts, I declined his kind offer, told him to fuck off, packed my bag and found my way to the nearest bus stop.

Standing outside the school, I though bloody hell what do I do now? I felt I had rather burnt my bridges, until in a burst of inspiration I remembered Jeremy, he who walks upon water, had attended the marine technical college in Southampton. Jumping on a Southampton bound bus I eventually found myself in the colleges St. Mary Street heavy engineering workshop. It was full of bits of ships, boilers, triple expansion engines and lots of official men in brown coats.

'What do you fucking want?' kindly enquired one brown coat. 'Hang on aren't you Jerry Tickner's brother? How the fuck is he? 'Yes I am, he's fine' I replied, 'and I'm looking for a ship's engineering course'.

'Well, you're in the right place' he said, and after conferring with the senior brown coat, I was given a really difficult entrance exam.

Memories of two plus two equals four, round pegs in square holes, and three times five is sixteen comes to mind as they passed me with distinction. Yes it was as easy as that. Thank heavens for elder brothers!

However dark clouds loomed on the horizon when my GCE results arrived. I had bombed out! Fortunately bullshit won through. The shipping company believed the 'lost exam papers story' and I signed up for a four year apprenticeship at the Southampton Marine Engineering College.

It's a fact that sometimes when you need a shoulder to cry on, as I did when I saw my exam results, help comes along from the most unexpected source. In the midst of my pal's jubilation at their exam successes, I was sitting on the sea wall of the Stone Sailing Club feeling downright sorry for myself.

The father of my pal Ox walked up, put his arm round me, and offered these words of advice. 'Some guys will pass every exam and win every prize going, and will still not be happy. You have other talents and skills that cannot be written down or tested, but believe me you will be successful'. Well the jury is still out on that one, but it helped me greatly at the time, mending a more than slightly dented ego.

So I had one final school summer holiday before joining the real world of gainful employment and I wanted to make the most of it.

My girlfriend had many redeeming features. She

was drop-dead gorgeous, sixteen, intelligent and lest I should forget, her family were loaded. I don't mean wealthy in the uncouth sense. I mean they lived in the posh part of Essex, and owned an agricultural machinery business. This produced machines that sprayed cow shit over fields. Whenever one was spotted by my beloved she would squeal in delight, 'Look Daddy another fur coat'.

One other example of their wealth was that, and please forgive this trivia, they had a waste disposal unit in their sink. Well, ok I know they are 'ten a penny nowadays', but back in 1969 they were as rare as rocking horse shit. It impressed me anyway.

My girlfriend and her sister used to wear long white shiny plastic boots with matching miniskirts, a great aid to penile gymnastics. Unfortunately the mum wore the same bloody boots; she looked like an older sister bless her.

Her parents suspected quite rightly that something more sinister than listening to records was happening between 'the apple of their eye' and 'the bit of rough from Hockley'. You bet your sweet arse there was, what a summer! I remember her folks going out for the day and leaving me and my mate the pilot to fornicate with the daughters spurred on by Simon and Garfunkel's album 'Bridge over Troubled Waters'.

'Making Love to Cecilia' was in full flight and I in mid stroke when I heard the sound of the 'rollers' tyres on the gravel path. Like a Brian Rix farce, I hopped to the bathroom, trousers around ankles, condom in hand. I pulled it over the tap, filled it full of water, and flushed it unceremoniously down the loo. This was the accepted form of disposal in the sixties. I buttoned up my shirt, hastily stuffed it into my trousers, and strolled nonchalantly downstairs to welcome them back.

Whilst enjoying a post-coital snack with the

mother, her father burst in and demanded to know what was floating in the top loo. Jesus I thought, didn't I flush the damn thing away? Fortunately the cause of his displeasure turned out to be a particularly fine specimen of a 'Richard the Third' which had swum back for a second viewing.

College Days

Jeremy showing me, the Pratt in a cap, a compass, Clan Ross Southampton docks 1970.

The long hot summer slowly slipped away and as always September was too soon upon us and I had become a student. After one final energetic exchange of bodily fluids with my beloved, my parents loaded me and my worldly possessions into the family car complete with my shiny new uniform blazer. 'You'll grow into it' my mother lied, as they despatched me down to my digs in Totton on the outskirts of Southampton and of course it never did fit.

I'm not sure what I expected from college life, the sixties had changed so much about society that it left the seventies with an impossible act to follow. So I started to smoke. How cool did we look strolling into a newsagent and ordering ten 'Number Six', even worse you could buy fags singly! They were so short that in two drags you were down to the filter!

Totton was miles from Southampton, taking hours on the bus as we poor first year students couldn't afford motorbikes or cars. The landlady's daughter got pregnant, just a coincidence you understand, so I moved out.

My next digs were in a terraced house in Shirley, the rough end of town, squashed in with five other students. The only rooms we were allowed to use were the bedrooms, but not during the day, the bathroom, and a room with six chairs, a table, and a coin operated fire grandly called 'the dining room'. Through a hatch in the wall, would arrive breakfast, bacon and eggs swimming in fat and 'something' with chips in the evening. Each Monday we would put our five pounds a week rent money in the hatch where it would be quickly snatched away.

In fact all we ever saw of our landlord was his tattooed right arm and hand during food delivery and rent collection.

We did, however, get to see considerably more of the landlady's daughter. Periodically, usually following a fight with her stepfather, she would burst into our room wearing a baby doll nightie, select one of our laps to plonk herself, and pour her heart out. After mollifying her, and after a tearful departure, we would compare erections. We didn't have access to a television, so you see any entertainment was welcome.

One of my cohabitants was 'a greaser', as bikers were then known, who rode a BSA 650 which you had to call a Beezer, on which he and I hurtled into college each day. He had all the gear, leather jacket emblazoned with a hells angel motif, tattoos, acne and long greasy hair. The short leather jacket worn over the uniform blazer rather spoilt the well 'ard image' as it looked rather like a pelmet. It wasn't easy to be the leader of the Shirley Chapter wearing something resembling a tutu.

Due to the absence of a TV in the digs, my mate Ken, who hailed from Newcastle, and I spent every evening in a pub where we contrived to make a half of bitter last all night, not an easy task I can tell you. I had never met a Geordie before Ken. It was six weeks before I could understand a word he said, and as the old saying has it, he was very well balanced with a chip on both shoulders!

The course curriculum consisted of Mondays, wearing a clean boiler suit, labouring in the heavy engineering workshop pulling apart bits of ships. The rest of the week spent in a classroom learning the theory of internal combustion and steam engines.

The first week was spent perfecting the use of a bastard file, I'm not blaspheming it's a type of file. I had a foreboding that this was going to be a very long apprenticeship!

Any thoughts of fun loving mini-skirted girl students to share our post tutorage hours were quickly dashed. We were affiliated to the hairdressing college that was full of delicate young men with pink 'floaty' scarves and velvet flares.

Southampton might have changed over the last twenty odd years but in those days, paint drying and grass growing observations were the top pastimes. A visit to the local common to watch the girls playing football, in the hope of a glimpse of white knickers, was deemed serious entertainment.

To keep our sanity, the boys and I used to frequent the Winston public house. I was one of the 'in crowd', mainly because I had let it drop that I drank with Jimmy Greaves, a famous Spur's and West Ham footballer. Well he did live next to my girlfriend and you might remember he was quite fond of the occasional tipple. Anyway the lads chose the Winston partly because it served a fine pint and because it was next to the Dell the Saints football ground but mostly because it was the 'local' for the girls of the Le Saints Union Convent.

Don't be put off by the name, these were guaranteed 'goers' provided you could prove you were a good Catholic boy. One line of the Catechism or the odd Hail Mary usually ensured you 'got your leg over'. One of the lads had a Ferrari key fob, which he would nonchalantly toss onto the girls drinking table with the offer of a lift home.

Good looking swine that he was, invariably the prettiest one with the shortest skirt would take up his offer. He then buzzed her home on the back of his Lambretta scooter, skirt up around her waist watched by the rest of us, a very appreciative audience. As I said entertainment was limited in Southampton in those days.

The Solent and Southampton Water has arguably the finest sailing in the South of England, infinitely better than the ditches and sand banks of the East coast where I had learnt to sail. So why in hell did I find myself, every Friday night running up the Avenue to hitchhike all the way back to Burnham-on-Crouch nearly the furthest East part of Essex. The power that a woman can exert over a man is incredible, hitching over three hundred miles every weekend just to get a 'legover'.

Another reason was that although Southampton was dull midweek it really took the biscuit on Saturdays and Sunday. It was best to be comatose in order to stop you doing dangerous things with sharp knives and wrists. One student actually threw himself off the university roof to escape!

A guy in the same year as me decided that he couldn't support his one pint a night of 'scrumpy' habit on his student's wages. He decided to commit an early version of a ram-raid. With meticulous attention he planned the date, shop, the item to be stolen, and the escape route. Friday night was chosen because the 'Old Bill' would be busy and the roads clear. His 'getaway' vehicle was overhauled, new brake blocks fitted and the chain oiled. Dressed in an inconspicuous orange boiler suit, woolly balaclava and wearing heavy-duty gardening gloves with a house brick in the pannier, he cycled through the shadows towards his target.

As it was August and a trifle hot, his attempt to travel unnoticed rather failed. However undeterred, and with a triumphant whoop, he picked up speed and hurled himself, the bike and brick, through the window of 'Jennings The Typewriter Centre Woolston Limited'. In a blur he seized the largest model, tucked it under one arm and sped off into the night.

The shops alarm quickly alerted the police and they gave chase. They had not counted on our hero's master plan. He had timed his escape to perfection, skidding onto the Woolston floating ferry just as the safety gates pulled shut. The police car screeched to a halt, siren wailing and blue lights flashing, its front wheels in the muddy waters of the Itchen watching impotently as the master criminal jeered as the ferry pulled away from the shore.

All was not lost however, for the forces of law and order. One small flaw in the typewriters thief's plan was the chain ferries maximum speed of three knots which allowed the police to drive over the adjacent bridge and calmly apprehend our man as the vessel docked.

The point of this story is to highlight to you how six

hours hitching was infinitely favourable to a weekend in Southampton as it could obviously drive a normally sane man to steal a typewriter and escape on a chain ferry.

Hitching is a fine art. We didn't go in for the modern practise of indicating ones choice of destination on a board. Instead we adopted the 'yearning yet wistful' imploring gaze at each prospective car closely followed by the 'fuck you' two-finger salute as the bastards drove callously by.

I had borrowed Jeremy's, quick glance to the East, uniform sailors cap which I lashed to my sail bag to indicate that here was a lonely sailor returned from the sea, please give him a lift home back to the bosom of his family, or any bosom in fact.

There was a code of practise which we hitching gentlemen of the road adopted, which was the first hitcher on the road gets the first lift. One Friday evening two mates and I were thumbing amiably away when an ancient lorry puffed to a halt. 'Room for two' shouted the driver, so I gallantly let the others jump on board, mainly as he was only going as far as Winchester, twenty miles up the road.

My patience was rewarded as shortly afterwards an Aston Martin DB 'something or other' screeched to a halt, reversed back to me and into its sumptuous leather interior I slipped. The driver, a BP tanker captain, had fallen for the uniform cap ruse. He didn't seem to mind my subterfuge in fact he even slowed down when shortly afterwards we passed the lorry carrying my mates, allowing me to flick the captains discarded cigar butts at them as we sped by.

After filling my head with more deep-sea adventures, my kind driver dropped me off at a West London tube station. Due to the paucity of my student grant I had to play the well known game of enjoying the hospitality of British Rail and London Underground at a highly subsidised rate i.e. Sod all!

To achieve this one ran through the barriers at high speed wearing an honest expression and eventually alighted at Stratford. Stratford was designed especially for penniless students who lived in Essex as one could walk calmly across the platform and board an over line train to the East coast with the attendant carnal proceedings to look forward to.

At your destination you watched carefully as the ancient BR ticket collector went about his business at one gate allowing you the opportunity to stroll casually up the steps of the bridge then run like Roger Bannister, showing my age now, down the other side through the unmanned gate to freedom. If your friendly ticket collector turned out to be a member of the Harriers track club and overhauled one, the fallback plan was to admit you had no ticket but had only travelled only one stop. I would tell the rather breathless collector I had boarded at Rayleigh four miles from Hockley my usual Friday night destination.

One word of caution, please study the railway timetable or note what stations you stop at when trying this ruse or you'll end up with a police record and I don't mean 'walking on the moon'. When I was eventually apprehended I calmly told the Nazi storm troopers better known as the ticket inspectors of Harold Wood that I had boarded at Guidea Park, which in their words would have been a fucking miracle. As in the celebrated Jethro joke, 'this train don't stop there Fridays'!

I'm not advocating you adopt free train travel as a pastime but how else could the student population get home?

As I commented earlier during the first week's bastard file lessons this was turning out to be a long apprenticeship. I couldn't wait for the weekends to perfect my thumbing techniques. I'd like to thank all the hapless motorists who had to listen to my flights of fancy as we sped up the pre M3 route to erotica lower Essex.

Fortunately, I could incorporate my brother's extensive fund of seafaring stories, all of this from a spotty, pale, barely out of nappies seventeen year old, which raised more than one disbelieving eyebrow.

I had a lot of fun and met a load of interesting people hitching excepting the time an uncle of one of my school friends insisting on giving me a lift home. As it was late and I couldn't spell paedophile let alone understood what it meant I jumped in.

After a couple of hours his hands started to wander as did his driving as we tussled our way down the windy country lanes, his hands on my testicles and mine on the door handle. A particularly fine uppercut to his bollocks seemed to reduce his ardour as I beat a hasty retreat. My favourite lift however was when a huge, ancient juggernaut hissed to a stop and high above me a door swung open, a distant voice urged me to 'jump the fuck up!' Throwing my bag complete with sailor's hat up into the cab I scrambled to meet my benefactor to be greeted by a giant, completely covered in tattoos and a beard that drooped over his steering wheel.

His name appeared to be 'fuck u', well that's what he had on his knuckles, but I'm pleased to report he loved his mother although her portrait tattooed on his arm in an attractive purple colour was slightly racy i.e. topless. An early version of Harry Potter's mate Hagrid comes to mind. He duly asked my destination as in you guessed it 'where the fuck are you going?'

He gunned the mighty beast up to about 90mph and asked me to keep my eyes peeled for the 'fucking bastard pigs', which I presumed, were the boys in blue.

Apparently when you drive rather large trucks the Highway Code is not applicable. Traffic lights, roundabouts and old ladies all went by in a blur but the best bit was when he grunted 'where had I been'? Realising that my phoney salty sea dog tales would not wash I said I had been away.

'What Dartmoor or the Scrubs?' he replied rather confirming my thoughts that he had known the inside of these government institutions.

I was very relieved to jump down in one piece straight into a pub for a medicinal calming pint of 'Watneys Red Barrel'.

My time in the Shirley digs had run its course, the landladies daughter ceased her plonking on laps so no more erection comparisons also their Himalayan mountain dog had turned the back garden into an extremely unpleasant excrement mountain.

A Jamaican college friend invited me to stay at Ma Snellings in Henstead Place central Southampton, central to a number of fine pubs I can tell you. This was paradise, no more sitting in a tiny back room; we had the run of the whole house, although I did rather take the piss when I rebuilt a motorbike in the kitchen sink.

Ma Snelling was a kindly widower who would do anything for her boys and took great comfort in her weekly visits to the local Catholic Church. We were astonished one evening on returning home after investigating the strength of a new real ale, to find Ma in tears. Sitting in the front room was a stony faced priest who had decided that as Ma's late husband was a Protestant the marriage was not legal and that SHE HAD BEEN LIVING IN SIN!

My Jamaican friend not understanding the complexities of the situation decided to eject the aforementioned Irish prick, not through the front door you would understand but through the sash window and what a satisfying noise it made too! To ensure the flying priest had completely grasped our displeasure at Ma's mistreatment I went out and helped him on his way with several goal kicks.

After rebuilding my motor bike in Ma's sink, it was a two stroke 250cc something or other, with no kick-start. I always parked it on hills to help bump start the sodding thing. I made the journey up to Essex, just the once as it was not the most reliable machine and bloody hard work. My girlfriends mother requested me to hide it in their garage in case the neighbours caught a glimpse, but full marks to her Dad he remembered his student days and roared off for a test drive.

Three hours later an oil sodden, mud splattered forlorn figure pushed my pride and joy back up the drive muttering something about the sodding chain falling off, shame.

Surfing Dudes

Eventually the academic year petered out and a letter 'poured in' inviting me to join the Clan Ross in Glasgow sometime in September. All that was left to complete my course was some work experience at Siley Weirs and Green a heavy engineering workshop in Tilbury.

I can remember sitting on a hundred foot lathe turning down a ships huge propeller shaft for two days bored senseless before reporting sick to enjoy the summer's rich tapestry of pleasures. As ever part of college life had involved exams and by an element of luck, hard work and I promise without cheating I had passed all subjects with flying colours, well if that didn't deserve some celebration I'm not a sailor.

Denese, me, Joff, Ox, Jerry and Jeremy

The sandy surf beaches of Jersey beckoned. Jumping a plane in Southend three Tickner brothers, Denese the girlfriend, my pal Ox and Jeremy's mate

Jerry Price with boards under arm descended on St Quoen bay. Father had furnished us with a tent. It was his camouflage one from the last fracas with the Germans with some obvious signs of wear. But hey! At least it was home.

Scrub Surf Dudes

The beaches were lined with blonde surf babes, the scrub land behind the sand dunes lined with not quite surf babes.

Guess which we ended up with! After a hard day falling off our boards, can't understand why. We had all the surfing attributes, long bleached hair, baggies and flip flops but alas no skills. We were quite good at being towed ignominiously back up the beach by the leashes as though the boards were dogs trying to get out of the water.

Anyway as us surfing dudes do we repaired to a lively bar and well Ox and I woke up in a two man tent which a) wasn't ours and b) had two men and two women in it. My pal with great glee chortled at my choice of companion until I invited him to look at his. Suitably chastened we decided to do the gentlemanly thing and did a runner.

Once back in the safety of our camouflaged world war two tent we realised with dismay that during the previous nights sexual Olympics we had mislaid, forgive the pun, some items of clothing and horrors there were the two girls, 'brummie' voices and all, talking to brother Joff outside. Seizing the initiative he told them we were gay, involved in a road accident, lapsed Mormons etc giving us just enough time to tear through the rotten fabric at the rear of the tent and escape. Having learnt our lesson we decided to imbibe more and fornicate less. Unfortunately on our last night we met some front of beach beauties who accepted our invitation for a meal, more a snack really, as funds were low. A detailed plan was constructed which involved ransacking our tent before dinner then inviting them back for coffee. Some of you are ahead of me I can tell. Well it went like clockwork, as we stood in front of our pile of canvas and bent tent poles my pals beau who was already holding his hand, gasped 'you must come back to our tent' and this was the crunch line 'you can't possibly sleep here' bingo!

Ox, me and Dads tent.

My companion wasn't quite as keen in fact as the other couple bounced off the tent walls and my bloody backside all night all I managed to remove was one of her three cardigans. So back home to the arms of my beloved and having protested undying love I left Upminster for the final time and set off for Glasgow, the gateway to my life at sea.

Zulu Wars

The Clan Ross

When we were kids the film 'Zulu' came to the local cinema each year. Father with his military background insisted we went to see it consequently we were word perfect with every scene and probably still are!

We also knew most of the choruses the Welsh sang whilst surrounded by thousands of Zulu's. Jethro thought they should sing something the Zulu's knew to stop them throwing them sharp spears, all of which came in handy when eventually I found the Clan Ross as it had Zulu crew.

With my travel instructions clasped in my mitt a somewhat subdued engineer cadet Tickner said a sad goodbye to his parents who were already planning to sell the house and boarded the overnight train to Glasgow. Arriving at eight in the morning I was surprised to see so many drunken people in Glasgow's Central station. Where did they get that much alcohol at this time of the day? A kind British Rail man speaking an unintelligible dialect which I presumed was Scottish advised I caught a bus to the docks so humping my sea chest, bag actually but sea chest sounds more authentic don't you think, I jumped on a bus.

Now I know nothing about football especially the Scottish variety so the sight of green scarfed people knocking shit out of red scarfed people viewed from the safety of the top of the bus was a tad confusing to this 'Sassenach'.

The docks hove into view, unfortunately the ports ship notice board was devoid of the whereabouts of the Clan Ross, in fact any Clan boats. A dock policeman could shed no light on the absent vessel or at least that's what I thought he said. So I did what any 'rufty tufty' sailor boy would do, I rang me Mum.

I felt sorry for the person at Clan Line head office who took my Mums call, Mrs T is not a woman to be trifled with where her boys are concerned.

A few minutes later the call box phone rang and a contrite voice informed me that the Clan Ross was delayed in Birkenhead and that I was booked into a hotel in Sauchiehall St for three days. Boarding the return bus I was pleased to observe our football friends were still using each other as punch bags, I like consistency, as I headed back to the city centre.

Glasgow in 1990 became the European city of culture, slums were knocked down and rebuilt elsewhere but in the late sixties it was dark, dirty and dangerous. Sauchiehall St was famous for vice and fights. So true to form, when I eventually found the dive shamming as my hotel two drunken brawlers were using the revolving doors as a boxing ring all very amusing until the glint of a knife alerted some passing police.

I locked my door securely that night. Naively not realising I was on expenses I smuggled burger and chips up to my room for three days until another head office call said they were picking up the tab and I was to join the ship tomorrow. Never being slow with the free lunch syndrome I discovered that seven pints of heavy, Scottish beer, accompanied by seven halves, large whiskies, enabled you to walk the Scottish way i.e. two paces forward and one back.

In the taxi to the docks in the morning things were more than a little blurred, and unfortunately without the weekends street fighting entertainment.

There she was at long last, the Clan Ross, built in 1966, a state of the art fruit ship and after all of one year at college I was going to help get her somewhere, destination still unknown. Climbing the gangplank with some trepidation I was met by a Zulu crewmember. Just what you would expect in a Glasgow dock, still all those years of watching that bloody film must have helped. On announcing my rank he kindly took me down into the engine room.

After walking around pumps, boilers and other big green things I realised engineers didn't necessarily sleep down below. Lugging my bag upward via near vertical steps I emerged, puffing slightly, into the officers accommodation and joy of joys I heard the unmistakable chink of glasses. One skill I have honed over the years is the ability to sniff out a bar. I was on home ground here! 'Officers Bar' the sign said, 'leave your rank outside'!

Pushing the door open I stepped into an atmosphere you could cut with a chainsaw, twenty pairs of eyes swivelled and pinned me to the wall. The inevitable question 'who the fuck are you?' they asked, 'engineer Cadet Robin Tickner' said I, a slight softening from the boys with purple stripes identified them as engineers. A long walk to the bar through an obviously stoned, bored out their skull set of officers nearly ended my career but why was the barman smiling at me?

'You'll be Jerry Tickners brother' said his friendly Welsh voice, 'I sailed with him on this very ship five years ago' and better still so had several of the inebriated officers. 'How is the old bastard?' And then in the time worn fashion of sailors the world over related some lurid details of runs up the road. The stories were helped along with copious quantities of foaming ale, Bacardi rum and orange then whisky and the rest is a blur. Someone showed me to my cabin where I undressed in a sort of hoppy way, hung my clothes neatly on the floor and sunk into oblivion remembering to thank once more the world for elder brothers.

An insistent ringing noise slowly filtered through what was left of my senses, a phone was jumping off its cradle next to a steaming cup of tea. Answering it a nice chap who apparently was the second engineer extended an invitation for me to view the engine room in my own time.

This was the life for me I thought as I slowly donned a pristine white boiler suit. A subtle knock announced the arrival of my steward a uniformed Zulu, they were everywhere, who rolled his eyes at me looked pointedly at his watch and suggested I should join the workers down below and disappeared with my still full tea cup.

In a daze I found a noisy door and slowly made my way down to 'Dante's Inferno', a cacophony of noise, dockside workers swinging bits of engine about and my new boss the second engineer not looking too happy.

Bollocking is too mild a word for my next ten minutes, how did I know we started work at eight and it was now eleven, not an auspicious start for me especially as the other engineering cadet a prick from Preston had been early on parade.

After a week I began to understand a little of shipboard etiquette, a cadet was the lowest of the low and the captain was God. The captain carried all the responsibility for the safety of the ship and all who sailed on her, and a cadet got pissed, actually in port everyone got pissed to make up for the dry times at sea.

I'm going to come clean here you may find in the following chapters several references to brothels which I in the interest of research have visited, by the way I have never gone to bed with an ugly woman, admittedly I have woken up next to hundreds, but view them as social clubs rather than houses of ill repute. That should keep my mother off my back.

I mention this as we sailed to Liverpool because there was a particularly fine example of a bordello staffed by ladies of the night all speaking in that pleasing Liverpool lilt, by the way what do you call a 'scouser 'in a suit?...the accused!

On our weaving return to the ship the participants of horizontal activity, not me, I have a beautiful girlfriend thank you, I just went to watch you understand, were issued with the Clan Line anti VD pack consisting of a wire brush and Dettol.

After two weeks of tramping around the coast loading cargo, spares, food, deep-sea crew and the third engineers wife our sailing orders arrived. Las Palmas for bunkers, or fuel for you non nautical types, then across the Bay of Biscay and down the African coast to Cape Town.

Leaving Southampton our ship sniffed the Ocean bowed to Neptune in the first sea roller and we were away, no more tearful phone calls and letters, we were alone, fifty souls on a little cargo ship ploughing its slow way to Africa.

In the Bay of Biscay, we were light ship which means no cargo so we were thrown all over the place. The stern got kicked out of the water at regular intervals causing the main engine to over speed and trip out. Everyone would then make a dash to the control room to reset and shove the fuel lever forward, a beer for the winner!

I loved the order of meal times, the set menu for the day of the week. Steak on a Sunday, a choice of curry every day with drinks in the tiny officer's mess before lunch and dinner. I also enjoyed the view from the dining saloon watching the Zulu deck crew getting washed about as we laboured through the giant waves of Biscay.

Another form of entertainment was watching the sweating steward's kick open the serving doors laden with huge trays of food. If the ship was on a downward roll they would roar across the saloon trying desperately to brake before cannoning into the bulkhead. If however it was on an uphill tilt they would trudge uphill like mountaineers. The best spectacle was a mix, uphill then down, them trays were like frisbees and doesn't food go a long way, it certainly bought a new meaning to silver service.

As we travelled further South towards where the butter melts we changed from our blue uniform into a natty little white outfit, shorts, long white socks, grey after washing with Marks and Sparks black socks, and short sleeved shirts replete with epaulettes. My pallid complexion, fresh in my seaman's book description, began to turn brown from off watch basting on the funnel deck and at last I began to find my way around the ship.

Sunset was my favourite time, leaning on the ships rail right at the stern watching out for the elusive green flash, still not seen thirty years later, as the sun dipped below the horizon and wondering how Albatrosses could follow the ships wake with so little effort for mile after mile.

Las Palmas for bunkers, topping up with cheap fuel with me and the off watch boys going up the road as a shore visit was termed. Las Palmas was famous in those days for cheap electrical goods, pizzas, proper ones from wood burning ovens and you guessed it, brothels. Well I was on a mission, like thousands of sailors before me I headed straight for the shops, emerging after some extensive haggling with a flash new Seiko watch and a music machine.

Stuffing a quick pizza I shot back to the ship as the Blue Peter was waving from the ships mast signalling our departure. Oh well I'll sample the ladies on the trip back I thought. One sting in the tail was that the whole crew had to be immunised against Black Death or something similar.

Unfortunately the doctor was unavailable so the local vet stood in for him. I think he was a dart player as he jabbed our arms with little finesse and not a single 'this won't hurt' comment still I don't suppose a good bedside manner is requisite when treating sheep. Ten hours later every man jack had a swollen arm and thumping headache.

It's a fact that sailors very rarely got sick because their mates would have to cover for them, unless you were a 'scouse 'engine room greaser when it was obligatory to go sick all the time, You may wonder why I have a down on our friend's from Liverpool. Well one chased me around an engine room with a bloody great spanner, pissed fortunately, and many years later I had a new car nicked in Liverpool, both good reasons I would suggest.

What do you call a 'scouser' in your living room? A burglar!

Two weeks later we rolled lazily around the Cape of Good Hope past Robin Island with Nelson Mandela incarcerated in its grim prison and onwards into Table Bay and my first African port.

Nothing had prepared me for Cape Town. Table

Mountain with its tablecloth of cloud dominates the whole city which nestles into the folds of its lower slopes. Call me naïve but I thought Africa was full of lions and elephants, natives in not much, preferably bare breasted and throwing spears.

Cape Town was a bit short of all these, what in hell was a Woolworth's doing in the high street. Jungles weren't supposed to have skyscrapers and where were the mud huts. Wilbur Smith had a lot to answer for.

On the other hand there were some great bars and for all I knew terrific houses of pleasure, but first stop was the Fireman's Arms men's bar just outside the docks. Dodging the ex Brit steam locomotives chuffing their way around the docks pushing and pulling the cargo wagons we found the bar.

Stuffing a buffalo size steak 'sarni' and supping my first of thousands of Lion lagers I pondered on why South Africans would have a public bar for men, a lounge for the ladies and a separate entrance and bar for blacks. This was my first experience of apartheid and what an eye opener it was.

I grew up in a small village in Essex where the only coloured faces manned the Indian or Chinese restaurants. A visit to London would expose you to West Indians in Brixton, Indians in Southall, Lebanese in the Edgware road, a whole Jewish community amongst others in Whitechapel in fact every nationality each equal in the eyes of God and the government. True, there were and still are racist bigots in Britain but a state that discriminated and segregated by the colour of your skin was profane. Quite rightly that was the view of most countries across the globe, many of which had imposed sanctions.

Separate beaches, toilets, park seats, shops, restaurants and sitting upstairs on buses. Apartheid pervaded every aspect of life making second class citizens of everyone without a white face and all this monitored by the most evil, ignorant police force imaginable.

As a young man walking around Cape Town a real pearl of a city in one of the world's most magnificent continents I felt devastated that man could be so inhumane. I was just a simple Essex boy with no experience of foreign countries and cultures but as my education in life continued I would witness far worse in other so called civilised countries. Political comment made let's go enjoy.

The off watch officers took a trip up Table Mountain in a rickety cable car, what a view. There was a dais on the top with distances to many major cities inscribed. It made me feel a long way from the bosom of my family until I turned around and fell over the feet of our family butcher. Maybe the world wasn't such a big place after all.

Back to the bosoms, family or otherwise, we had been at sea for several weeks, where was the action. Well you could go up Lions Head, an adjacent peak to Table Mountain and shag a willing Cape Coloured prostitute. These poor girls were both beautiful and universally discriminated against for being half caste. That didn't stop many hypocritical whites who took their pleasure there.

In the suburbs of Cape Town was a shantytown for blacks called 'District Six' supposedly a teeming den of vice. We took a trip there in a taxi, stayed for one nano second and got out fast!

As we have the Irish as the butt of our so called humour, South Africa has the Afrikaner's, notably a Mr Van De Merwe.

There is a story about Van having a very liquid evening and waking up in District Six. Either side of him were two corpulent very black ladies, getting caught was a shooting offence, not for whites they would get their wrists slapped the girls would get shot! Climbing carefully over one of the girls she woke and cried 'not me baas, you married the other one'.

I got to know Cape Town, the windy city much better through the years but we had finished unloading and were once more on our way. Port Elizabeth was our next stop. A small port with the unenviable reputation of being the abortion capital of South Africa, hence the expression 'I'm going to see my Auntie in PE'. I'm afraid I was to experience the town's trade some years later.

East London came next, now we are talking serious shanty town here, it was a town of two halves divided by a bridge, and in my view our stay there nearly became a bridge too far!

Our cargo plans were running late so we were granted the dubious pleasure of a weekend in the fleshpots of the town. Booze on British cargo ships ran very cheap, a gallon of lager took about ten pence out of your funds so a few liveners always preceded a run up the road.

When the legs had gone weak it was time to go, fall down the gangplank into a taxi guided by one of the old hands who would know a suitably seedy nightclub. This particular night we found ourselves the wrong side of the bridge in cowboy country i.e. let's get the flock out of here. Things were looking more than a little 'iffy' when an Indian beckoned us into a squalid excuse for a hotel. Stumbling in he indicated that we could stay the night as no taxis would dare into the area until dawn. Six very drunk men in two double beds was a bit tight but when our friendly porter sent two scantily clad black ladies carrying yet more booze things got positively obscene.

As you remember I was in love so I slept in a

wardrobe until one of my shipmates mistook my quarters for the heads, kind of him I thought wetly. We got thrown out at day break leaving our lady friends to comment 'why for last night you call us African princesses but this morning tell us to fuck off and kick our dogs'. Once again the purser in his other role as ships doctor issued several VD kits; smugly I was not a recipient.

Durban with big waves breaking over its outlying banks greeted us with searing sunshine and for a reason best known to themselves, Zulu's in full ceremonial costume riding rickshaws.

Durban is one of my favourite cities, it's near the tropics so has a great, somewhat humid climate, but it just bounces. Great hotel bars, nightclubs, white sandy beaches with amazing surf and a nurse's home right next to the docks.

There were two main beaches, South beach for whites boasting a shark net and North beach for blacks which didn't, says it all really. Durban was truly cosmopolitan, if possible within the apartheid regime.

I saw a very famous female black singer in Durban performing to a white audience, it was only later I discovered she had been awarded an honorary white citizenship for the show!

Part of my cadet's education was to visit the Durban Merchant Navy officers club, so dutifully dressed up wearing a tie, a stipulation of ladies bars, we fell into taxis after the usual imbibing in the ships bar. I can't remember much about the night, I know the club had steps because I fell up them to cut a fine arrival and probably down them on departure as well.

When I awoke it was to a vision of pink, sort of how you would imagine Barbara Cartland's boudoir to be. Next to me was Jill as she kindly introduced herself and how shall I put this she was as nature had brought her into the world and there was a lot of her. Not to be accused of too much detail, six pounds of wet liver, see wedding night first wife, and butcher shops came to mind.

The bedroom door was flung open and another complete stranger, her mother Betty it transpired, said breakfast was ready. Retrieving my clothes from around the room I dressed and joined the ladies and a slightly swarthy Greek looking gentleman for breakfast. I had a hurried poached egg, toast, juice and tea before bidding hasty goodbyes to Jill and Betty and escaped back to the ship.

Harry the purser grabbed me into his cabin and slammed the door. 'Are they here?' he whispered, eyes rolling with fear, 'who?' said I, 'Clan Line Betty and Jill the Pill' he replied. 'You mean those friendly ladies have done this before?' I asked a picture of naivety. Every fucking night since Pontius got his pilot's licence and it appeared Harry was one of their conquests, hence his hiding.

'What did you get for breakfast' was his next question, not realising the relevance I told him to which he nodded sagely and said 'not a bad score'.

It was only a week later when I had compared notes with two further recipients of Jill's charms that I realised her scoring system. A short arsed frail electrician off a banana boat got a boiled egg for his nights exertions and a giant of a third mate, hung like a horse, well so he boasted, who got a full English breakfast and a return invitation. And you ladies call us sexist!

The ladies came back to haunt me on a subsequent visits.

A company letter arrived for the Captain, a man who spent little of his time sober in port and was not much better at sea. Its contents must have seemed a godsend. We were to complete discharging our cargo up the East African coast, Mombassa, Lorenzo Marques now known as Maputo and Beira. We would then return to Durban where the ship would lay up for several months awaiting the start of the new fruit season.

Half the crew would be sent home but the cadets would stay on to gain valuable experience in engine maintenance. I had mixed feelings, part of me wanted to go home to my loved one but the other half was already intoxicated by Africa and the sailor's life.

Mombasa

We tramped up the African coast. I was reading Wilbur Smiths books, which came alive as we experienced the places, the people and the feel of the country he portrays so well. The temperature and humidity climbed and I now had the colour of the natives, I always thought Dad had a bit of tarbush in him. The Zulu crew looked on with wry amusements as the young 'Sahib' toasted in the noon day sun.

Now brother Jeremy had indicated that 'Mombers', as us salty sea dogs called Mombasa was probably the best run ashore on the African continent and we were up for it. After a very sweaty week at anchor, the Kenyans, having let half the Russian fleet alongside before us, tugged us into the port.

The sounds, smells and general melee of steam trains, honking tugs and swinging cranes bowled you over. The vibrant colours of the teeming dock workers attire and the pervading pungent smells of spices meant this could only be Africa.

Now many of you have probably lain on a beach or bounced about on a Kenyan safari but thirty odd years ago tourism was in its infancy. Very elite, not a package holiday in sight. The Kilindini road with its archway of tusks and rows of seedy bars was a mecca for the drunken sailor.

Our Chief engineer was a fine man, unflappable in a crisis, he worked his boys hard but there was always a case of beer in the engineer's mess after a long day's work. He decided that as a special treat for the new boys he would show us the sights of the glittering city.

Bolstered with ten pints of Clan Lines best lager we boarded the local transport, which turned out to be mini mokes! Somehow we found the red light district and on mass poured into a series of bars complete with loud music and exotic under clad ladies stripping on STILTS!!!!

The chief engineer stood several rounds, good man that he was until he counted his companions. Finally realising all the engineers were present he enquired, 'who the fuck is night on board'? 'the fucking deck officers' we replied! We thought it funny anyway. The chief seemed to have lost interest in shipboard etiquette at that time as his eyes crossed, breath went ragged and his fists clenched the tablecloth. The reason for his displeasure, actually pleasure became apparent when the sound of a zip returning home and the wiggling out from under the table by one of the dancers confirmed that rank does have its privileges.

Now as I have stated many times I was in love, with no thoughts of carnal activities, however these girls were getting prettier by the pint even though they had this alarming habit of chucking peanuts at me and the prick from Preston calling us "cherry boys" which apparently meant virgins. Bloody cheek!

As the beer was consumed, one by one my companions fell under the spell of these African beauties and disappeared into the night. I stood by my principles, actually I fell by my principles as the night was old and the beer was strong,

I woke to find myself in a dilapidated taxi bouncing through the jungle accompanied by the fourth engineer who appeared to be stuck to a dusky maid by the mouth and by the waist, well groin really. Thanking my fellow officer for saving me from the bar he informed me we were going to a real up market house of ill repute, the only two-storey brothel in Mombasa. Wow did I feel honoured.

Clutching my principles I lurched into the taller than usual mud shack with a deluxe thatched roof and watched as my pal negotiated with his new girlfriends parents the price of shag. I recall the princely sum of two Rand, a packet of biscuits for Mum and a beer for Dad, oh and a corner for me to kip in.

Now there was a sister who stumbled over me later, who out of the kindness of her heart invited me upstairs, just for coffee, please understand, as I could barely stand let alone talk. When I awoke it was pitch black with just a pale shaft of moonlight filtering through the straw roof. One small problem, I don't recall living in a thatched hut, so where in hell was I? Who was I in bed with? And how could she snore and fart with such perfect pitch and resonance? I vaguely remembered a taxi ride unfortunately that still didn't give me a clue as to my present whereabouts. As an 'aide memoir', my corpulent and somewhat flatulent companion belched and rolled over; exposing a haircut you could play noughts and crosses on.

In the slow light of dawn the large orange hairy spider turned out to be the red wig 'my lady of the night' had worn earlier, which she had casually hung on a nail before throwing me onto her rude bed.

The pressure on my bladder screamed for relief, so quietly falling out of bed I donned my shirt, socks and pants. Where in hell were my trousers and wallet? Well there was sod all left in that anyway.

I found the exit. Groping along the wattle walls I realised that a clean flush loo had not been included in the architect's plan so finding a very dark corner I began to urinate copiously. All was not well with my choice of toilet, as it suddenly became an open doorway with me pissing over the freshly woken occupant's feet, an extremely large black chap.

Wishing him good morning over my shoulder I thundered along the passageway screaming for help and cannoned into my sleeping partner who was complaining about her lack of pay. As I had not taken part in any fornication, too much alcohol is a great contraceptive, I continued on my way followed by the aggrieved large black chap and a naked wigless lady.

But help was at hand, our friendly taxi driver had waited for his charges and shouted up at me. He was enjoying the show. 'Jump!' the bastard said, 'fuck off!' I replied, but seeing as my pursuers were getting nearer I pulled myself over the small wall and fell to the ground.

Well they say that babies don't hurt themselves when they fall and neither did I as I executed a fine parachute landing rolling over in the dust resplendent in my Marks and Sparks truth be told rather soiled knickers. Jumping into the waiting taxi I hurled abuse at the pursuing couple and slapping the driver on the back gave the Clan Ross as my destination.

All was not well with the car ignition however, as the starter motor failed to kick the engine into life despite frantic twisting of the key. The cars lack of movement and probably my insensitive comments spurred my would be assailants back into life. As they clattered down the stairs I jumped out and pushed that sodding taxi down the road.

Fortunately the driver was up with bump-starting and finally the reluctant engine burst into life with me hanging grimly on. I sometimes feel that I was an early version of Indiana Jones and that Spielberg owes me a percentage from Raiders of the lost Ark!

Upon my return to my ship the purser who was manning the gangplank wished me good morning, and pressed a Clan Line anti VD pack into my hand, 'not needed' I replied sanctimoniously.

Perhaps I should tell you a little more about my floating home which I shared with my fellow white officers and sundry crew.

The Clan Ross was a relatively modern ship; she

had a Sulzer main engine with overhead exhaust valves and Rolls Royce turbo generators.

Big as a block of flats the engine room had four levels, the middle level housing an air-conditioned control room. State of the then art of automatic controls allowed us to go unmanned at night so day work for all engineers.

The second, third and fourth engineers had an alarm panel in their cabins which gave them about one minute to wake up and throw on a towel then run to the boiler room door, slide down the engine room rails into the control room and sort out the emergency. Not an easy task when you are deep in the land of nod.

Bruv and me, Cape Town

The Clan Ross was one of the last ships to be

constructed for the British and Commonwealth shipping company, she had three sister ships, the whole family known as the R boats.

They were the first semi-automated automated ships fortunately backed up by hand control as they were always breaking down.

Hot water was supplied from a donkey boiler in the funnel and starting air and pressure for the toilet system came from a bank of compressors. We enjoyed the luxury of an air conditioned control room and clean workshop complete with a storeroom full of spares; you can't exactly pop into Halfords for a new fuel injector in the middle of the Indian Ocean!

The hatches were of the Macgregor type not the 'batten down the hatches Jim lad' of older ships, serviced by derricks which could run on steam in an emergency. Some of these technical bits of ship paraphernalia play a part in this story. Any engineering anorak who wants more detail I suggest you bugger off down to the maritime museum or local library and bore the arse of their inmates.

Accommodation was by rank, the more senior you were the higher your cabin, thus the Chief Engineer, Captain, Mate and sparky, by default, radio officer to you, lived on the top deck facing 'for'd'. Down a level in cabins also facing 'for'd' lived the Purser, second engineer and second mate whilst the rest of us minions were scattered in cabins along the ships sides. We cadets being the lowest of the low were lucky not to berth in the bilges!

The ship boasted a spacious saloon facing aft, where as previously mentioned, in stormy weather we could watch the hapless crew being washed about the deck, very conducive to aid ones digestion. Just near enough was the officer's bar complete with draught Tennant's at five old pence a pint and a selection of 'fall down' juices or spirits as you land lubbers say, also keenly priced.

The engineers had a duty mess complete with a metal table where we would lounge resplendent in oil soaked boiler suits drinking tea and enjoying a well earned 'smoko'. You may wonder why I mention the metal table. Well as entertainment was in short supply we would amaze the young Zulu stewards with white man's magic.

As the poor soul reached for the brimming metal ashtray an engineer with a magnet in his hand under the table would move it out of his reach. An early form of the Ouiji board perhaps, well it frightened the shit out of the Zulu's and kept us amused, perhaps we should go out more?

Up top was a games room with a dart board and table tennis table, both lethal in any kind of seaway. Cannoning off the bulkheads trying to return an ace serve or skewering your opponent with an errant dart would have today's health and safety Johnnies running for their clipboards.

Every Saturday the engineer cadet i.e. me or the prat from Preston, would show a movie. This was long before video or DVD's, it was Bell and Howell reel to reel technology a mini version of a cinema projector. In the tropics we would sit the officers on the bridge deck the crew on the hatches and project the film onto a tarpaulin strung between derricks.

In colder climes we would view in the cramped comfort of the officer's bar the latest Hollywood offering which were always over ten years old.

This unfortunately necessitated a second showing for the crew deep in the bowels of the ship.

Forgive me, I forgot to mention the crew's cabins well they were aft and low, ships were designed with apparently with no thought of crew comfort. Their galleys one for deck and one for engine crew were right aft on the stern deck alongside their rather rudimentary toilet facilities. One of my tasks each morning was to dip the crew's galley oil tanks which fuelled their stoves. Clambering up on top of their galleys I had to wrap a diesel soaked rag around my face to hide the atrocious smell of drying fish which was served with our daily curries. Filling a car in a petrol station still brings back memories of their galleys!

My naval architecture memory is a bit hazy on exact ships plans, so just in case some smart arse ex Clan Line nerd feels the need to correct me bugger off I can't remember!

So who sailed these great black hulled ships with two red stripes on their funnels?

I could say a bunch of drunks whiling their time away until the next run ashore, but that would be unfair. Generally they were extremely talented, highly experienced, professional time served drunks whiling their time away until the next run ashore.

The officers consisted of, the Captain, he who should be obeyed and carried the can for everything, the mate in charge of navigation, the second mate responsible for cargo, third mate responsible for drinking and running off with my first wife, more details later, and sundry deck cadets.

So the above pointed the ship to various destinations, wearing crisp white uniforms and lounging about in the air conditioned bridge whilst the real hero's of this story, the engineers, toiled below in Dante's inferno or in the engine room as it was better known. You might have noticed a slight favouritism towards our grimy friends, oil and water never mix, it's a historical thing!

The Chief Engineer carried the responsibility of getting the ship from A to B. I admired most of the chiefs I sailed with as they were of the old school, time served engineers rather than fresh faced university bods. We also carried a second, a junior second, third, fourth and junior engineers plus a couple of cadets.

Oiling and greasing the engines were a team of Zulu donkey men who also served the worst tea in the world to the engineers on watch.

Deck work was undertaken by the deck crew who were responsible for chipping, painting, warp handling and anchoring. Anything that didn't move was covered in good old Clan Line black paint.

By the way they say you could always tell a Clan boat by shouting Jock down the engine room skylights and if an 'Aye what the fuck do you want?' floated back it was one of ours.

Another lucky bastard who made the correct career decision was the purser, he of the never let a backhander get away. His cabin positioned at the top of the gangplank was ideally suited to snare any unwary supplier or corrupt customs officer with liberal amounts of alcohol before extorting his 10% commission.

Harry was my first and best purser, 'lower than the belly of a snake' his favourite description of port authorities who failed with the 'acckers'!

Before the age of sat phones and mobile phone technology in fact for many years after the invention of steam radio, ships had huge green machines with wires, diodes and aerials. These monsters were manned by the sparky who communicated with the outside world saying over and out, roger and hopefully not Mayday much like the gay crew from the film 'Airplane', and the lucky bastard only worked four hours a day. We also boasted a 'lecky', who understood wires, volts, amps and other electrical terms, he also kept the lights and the beer cooler running so he was very important. Last and least was the 'Chippy'. Now on a white-crewed ship he was crew but he would have stuck out a bit sitting amongst all the Zulu's in their mess so he was an honorary officer on the Clan Ross.

The 'Chippies' Story

I cannot move on without telling you more about this extraordinary character. For a start he looked like Popeye complete with a pipe which he smoked upside down when it rained. He also had a deep hatred for gentlemen of a different hue. This dislike was based on an incident when some Suez Canal 'Gilly Gilly' men dropped a ships lifeboat on his head which also accounted for his slightly glazed expression.

I should explain, just in case your ship experienced problems on passage through the Suez Canal you had to carry local boatmen known as 'Gilly Gilly' men to row lines ashore thus securing the vessel. Their more usual pastime was trying to rob you! Anyway due to this lifeboat incident our 'Chippy' tried at all times, well to kill or at least maim Abduls, not in a vindictive manner more as a 'Holy Grail'.

Whilst tramping around India Clan boats would anchor off the coast and wait for native dhows to sail out and tie up alongside. Their crew would discharge cargo using steam driven derricks and lived on deck eating rice cooked on galvanised dustbin lids over charcoal fires.

Toilet facilities had to be provided which is where our 'Chippy' enters the fray. He would build a timber thunder box complete with seat and excrement aperture and fit it hanging off the aft deck. Picture the scene, Mr Patel wanting to exercise his normal morning ablutions clambers into the thunder box clutching his tin can full of water in lieu of loo paper, excuse the pun and in his other hand a copy of the local newspaper.

Settling down to commune with nature he little realised his fate. With one swift tug of a rope 'Chippy' operated a trapdoor sending poor Patel complete with paper, tin, and excrement to the shark infested Indian

Ocean waiting below.

Local thieves unaware of our lunatic woodworker's murderous practises would paddle out under the cover of darkness and shin up our anchor chain for expected rich pickings. Earlier 'Chippy' would lay out some steel reinforced flexible steam pipes and then hide up in great expectation, once the thieves were sighted steam would be cracked on.

So what happened, well the steam pipe operates like a garden hose when no one is holding it except superheated steam not water engulfs the hapless victim and the steel pipe whips him to a gory mess.

Not content with possible drownings, shark attacks or severe garden hose type injuries he had one last trick up his sleeve.

What happens when circus animals get too old to work? They ship them out to South African game parks where they can run and play and jump through hoops in their natural environment. Guess who shipped them and guess who cared for the animals, Clan Line and 'Chippy'. We carried giraffes in horseboxes with holes for their necks, lions, and on one occasion a particularly evil tempered baboon.

Now 'Chippy' and the baboon had something in common they both hated the Indians. The poor creature was chained to a stake giving him a small circle of freedom on the foredeck. The crew quickly worked out the extent of travel and would stand just outside the danger area and taunt the beast.

'Chippy' let them get confident then secretly lengthened the chain. What a surprised group of Indians the purser treated in the ships sick bay that night, 'Chippy' had struck again.

An Engineers Tale

I mentioned earlier some mechanical bits, funnels, overhead valves and the like, so without turning this passage into a technical journal I'd like to recount some adventures in engine room land.

A stay in port gave the engineer's time to maintain or stick back together pieces of the engine that were in need of tender loving care much like your car needs a service when you remember or can afford it. With a slightly tender head after a night on the town or rumble in the jungle I was informed that the exhaust valve to the boiler was jammed. This was a huge butterfly valve that diverted the main engine exhaust gasses through a bloody great pipe to heat the boiler instead of having to burn fuel oil.

The operation consisted of strapping a small cadet into a harness and lowering him through a manhole down to the offending valve and lightly adjusting it with a sledgehammer. Slightly concerned for my safety I requested a viewing of the lifting gear. A large Zulu with gloves on was brought forth, not a chain block in sight.

Now in subsequent years I sailed with all nationalities of crew, Indians, Pakistani's, Chinese and white crew. The worst were our fellow Brits, mostly drunken 'scousers' and as mentioned earlier, one even chased me round the 'genny' room with a wheel key due to a request for him to stop sleeping on the job!

Fasting for Ramadan always weakened the western gentlemen, you would stumble over them dehydrating in the boiler room. The best crew by far were the Zulu's, conscientious, willing, hardworking and immensely proud of their heritage they were a great bunch. So I had no fear except for paranoid claustrophobia whilst knocking shit out of that valve with just one man wearing gloves dangling me in mid-air.

After a few days of maintenance and a few more nights of decadence we steamed out of Mombasa bound for Lorenzo Marques a former Portuguese colony now known as Maputo after the Frelimo mercenaries won back their country for the disappointed locals.

Maputo was reputed to be as bad a night out as Mombasa so I had high hopes. One of our sister ships had even had her wooden faced bridge machine gunned as it entered port by some high spirited soldiers.

After patiently waiting at anchor as Chinese ships barged the queue we finally came alongside to the usual cacophony of tugs, cranes, steam trains and the general bustle of dock life. The padre from the local seamen's mission came down to save our souls and invited us back to his club for a game of football. These missions provide a refuge for sailors to get up to the minute religious advice and keep them away from the local fleshpots.

What he failed to inform us was whom we were going to play. As we rounded the bend into his compound we saw a large group of camouflage clad Frelimo soldiers kicking a ball about using their machine guns as goalposts. Not surprising we lost about hundred to one, with some very sporting fouls on their part. The idiot who scored our solitary goal was chancing his arm in my opinion.

Escaping the Christian clutches of the padre we sallied into town, a once well maintained Portuguese place with wide boulevards and fine houses now slipping into sad decay as money was siphoned off to support the war. We found a house of ill repute and as usual mislaid some of the boys but eventually fell into a great bar resembling a Wild West saloon complete with bar mirrors and a honky - tonk piano.

All was well until some lads from our rival company Bank Line made an appearance. The ensuring brawl would have made John Wayne proud, bodies sliding along the bar, bar stools over heads and drunks through windows into the main street. We beat a hasty retreat when some large men in uniform arrived with very mean looking truncheons. After viewing the local jail, pits in the ground topped with metal grids the next day I felt it was probably the right move.

We had experienced some problems with our air pressured toilet systems so we fine tuned the system so it had just the right power to gently blow away the waste. We also knew the Captain had a shit every morning at nine so an engineer would stand by ready to jack up the pressure at the appropriate time.

A very satisfying roar of air, urine and human waste not to mention the wail of a shit sodden captain was in some way compensation for his bad attitude.

Not that we could do it every day, mores the pity. At last the final cargo was dropped onto the dusty dock and we were away to civilisation South African style for our lay up.

On arrival in Durban we were tugged and pushed into Point Road dock a rough part of town away from the main port area. A major benefit, after avoiding a severe mugging getting out of the dock, was how close we were to South beach with the Addington Hospital's nursing home only a few minutes stagger.

After saying sad goodbyes to the departing crew even sadder that the Captain wasn't going with them, the remaining band soon settled into an easy routine. We were plugged into shore power, which meant the generators were not used so no watches for the engineers, yippee! Day work only and every weekend off. I was torn between wanting to see more of the world or staying in a vibrant surf city with some of the world's most beautiful beach babes, I didn't stay torn for long!

A few days into our stay I had a call from the Chief engineer to say there was a friend of mine on the dock. Well the only person I knew in Durban was 'Jill the Pill' so with some trepidation I peered over the ships side to see, joy of joys my great pal Ox standing there. Rushing down to grab him and then rushing down several Lion lagers we got up to date.

He was taking a sabbatical from making millions in the British property market staying with some of his relative's sixty miles inland in Pietermaritzburg after travelling out on an Italian cruise liner. He was working in a male boutique called 'Pants Plus' and good looking bastard that he was making some extra rand by modelling. He and I were pals from sailing on the east coast of England, we learnt to sail, drink and screw over many happy years.

As befitting surf dudes, as we were to become, he had beads around his neck and hair to his navel well that's what our drunken Captain said as he ordered this hippy off his boat.

Fortunately Harry the ever smiling Purser had taken a shine to Richard 'so bollocks to the Captain' he said, 'you're welcome anytime and you can have the best food on the ship served in Robin's cabin'. True to his word that's what happened every happy weekend for the next few months.

So I had my best pal down every weekend, pulling engines apart during the week and out on the razz every night but there was one cloud on my horizon, no letters from the love of my life back home.

Then one day a very thin missive arrived mistakenly addressed to a bloke called John, well it opened with Dear John anyway. She had found a new man, so after a nano second of grief well actually quite a few days, I realised I was free so I sportingly put her letter on the ships notice board and invited comment.

When sufficient comments had been made I posted it back, childish I know but I was spurned!

Smoking 'Rambo' engineer

Ox or Richard Oxley to give his full title, purchased a decrepit Volkswagen kombi so loved by us surfers in which we threw our newly acquired boards to enjoy shark dodging or surfing as is better known on or more often under the perfect waves of South beach.

His board was a natty little blue number with three fins. I had acquired mine after a strenuous encounter with a surf loving Addington nurse. Happy days lying on the beach next to the 'Picking Chicken' beach bar with various sun tanned females and evenings spent on the town in great bars. Such a far cry from the rain drenched beaches of Britain in winter or summer in fact!

Ox and me surfing South Beach

Some weekends he would bring his pal Tom down in which case Ox would share my bed and Tom the couch. This rather surprised my Zulu steward who on bringing my morning cup of tea thought I had turned gay and had a spare boy just in case.

Durban was a little like I imagined America to be, wide streets, single storey shops and my first taste of fast food, excepting the good old Wimpy bars of England.

The city was a mixture of people and cultures, whites owned the shops, Indians ran them and blacks cleaned the streets. Adding to this strange racial mix came thousands of holidaymakers. Afrikaners with their guttural baby Dutch language and the occasional European, eyes opened to the effrontery of the apartheid regime.

Throw in scorching heat, blue skies, beaches to die for, the soul of Africa and you had a heady mix, a powder keg just waiting to explode. In hindsight that's what happened despite Mandela's efforts this most beautiful country is still reeling from one crisis to another.

All this was of no importance to a young sailor, we just worked and played hard. Every weekend we would throw a Clan Ross party, inviting the stalwart nurses from Addington, members of the Merchant Navy Officers club and sundry females met in bars, beaches and shops.

Clan Ross party

I now had a girlfriend from the navy club who would always tut when Jill the Pill hove too with me pretending not to know her, a bit difficult when Jill winked knowingly and said hello Robin. This girlfriend, her Mom and Dad always came to the ships parties, mainly because the Mother was enjoying the affections of the first mate!

Late one night she arrived flustered from a liaison, covering her mouth, apparently too much drink had passed her tonsils and whilst praying to the porcelain God she lost her false teeth.

Incidentally allegedly isn't a blowjob extra when they take their teeth out.

Our friendly Purser rushed to the sick bay to source a spare pair and for a whimsy solemnly handed them to the poor woman explaining the engineers had found them in the toilets u bend, her smile was a bit crooked for weeks after.

One weekend tired of the sights of Durban, Richard, Tom and I planned an excursion to Eshowe in Zululand to experience the real Africa, to absorb their culture and to ogle at the tits of the traditional Zulu war dancing maidens, see the film Zulu and you will know what I mean.

The old Kombi groaned its way up into the hills passing suit clad Zulu's wearing what looked like bowler hats striding along beside the highway bound for who knows where, church perhaps, it was a Sunday.

Eventually at lunchtime, steam hissing from the radiator we arrived in Eshowe a one-horse town if I ever saw one. There was a tumbledown hotel boasting a full Sunday menu for ten Rand, a little excessive but we had to eat as in South Africa you couldn't get a drink on a Sunday unless you were dining.

Supping an aperitif, three pints of Castle lager we repaired to the games room where a dead snooker table resided surrounded by Aspidistra plants, it was like a scene from the last days of the British Raj.

Midst break we were forcibly ejected by several large South African police who informed us it was illegal to play sport on a Sunday, what a country. Replete with a fine lunch we saw the tits, heard the music and hurried back to Umlanga rocks for some surfing, so much for culture.

Many years later for Dads eightieth birthday brother Joff took Dad up to London to listen to the curator of Rourkes Drift museum speak about the Zulu uprisings. Sadly the curator was murdered just recently.

South African police as described so ably by Tom

Sharpe were a rule unto themselves. They specially trained dogs to rip the throats out of blacks and would give a speeding ticket to a white errant motorist who had unfortunately run over a black family whilst driving totally pissed, well it's not easy is it?

And the uniform, well picture this, the typical cop had eyes too close together peering out of a Neanderthal skull crowned by a massive peaked hat that reached to the chin. Slightly stooped, as they hadn't quite finished evolution they bore a striking resemblance to the more backward species of monkey. A crisp massively over starched Nazi type shirt and shorts covered their frame, the shorts just brushing their shins with long socks reaching their testicles bottomed off by shiny jackboots, they made an arresting sight.

Driving back to the ship we were treated to another fine example of South African authority, this time in the form of the railway police. As steam locomotive buffs would know we sold many of our old British Railway 'choof choofs' to the South African port authorities where they spent their last days shunting goods wagons around the docks.

The poor old Kombi shuddered to a halt across some railway tracks and despite furious twisting of the ignition key refused to budge. A loud knock on the driver's window alerted us that a large talking hat wanted our attention. Railway police wore the same attire as the cops. Winding down the window we were informed in a thick Afrikaner accent that 'you can't park your car here' which was fucking obvious as a type O locomotive was huffing its way towards us.

Fortunately several workers were passing by and in their usual good natured way pushed us away from disaster, it was the fastest the old Volkswagen went for quite some time.

Engine room work was not all muck and bullets,

sweat and grease, there was some fine adjustments to be made to the head gear i.e. the afore mentioned poppet valve and I don't mean a term of endearment.

Imagine if you will an exhaust valve like the one on your car only six feet tall, well just like your old car they are driven by cams with tappets to be adjusted. As the valves were six foot the clearance was probably pro rata an inch which was set using a three foot aluminium feeler gauge and they had to be set whilst the engine was turning!

One engineer Jeremy and me Clan Ranald 1970

Stretch your imagination a tad more and picture the sight of the chief engineer sticking the massive feeler gauge in the gap between valve and tappet with two cadets tightening the nuts with oversize spanners all going slowly up and down. Just like a scene from a Buster Keaton movie escaping on one of those manual railway carts!

A month into our stay in Durban the Clan Ranald

berthed alongside complete with Jeremy my eldest brother as third engineer so two Tickners were laid up in Durban. Could it get worse for the locals?

Yes! Every six weeks brother Joff, third purser on the Windsor Castle pulled into port. Eager to sample the delights of the flagship of our fleet Jeremy and I resplendent in home laundered slightly grubby uniforms sped on-board into the splendour of Joff's cabin. Red shades on the lights, posters on every wall including the classic tennis girl scratching her arse, drinks cabinet and a giant sound system.

Joff me and Jeremy, Windsor Castle

This wasn't a cabin it was cross between a disco and a bordello, posh words for you know what, and anyway mother will have stopped reading this drivel by now and probably disowned me.

Joff. Clan Ross and Ranald in background

The Windsor Castle had woman, bars, a disco, cinema, swimming pools, lifts, stewardesses, mostly dykes unfortunately, cabins full of woman oh have I mentioned that already and only six weeks per trip with ten days off.

I decided there and then that when I went back to sea after finishing my exams 'passy' boats were for me, and so it came to pass.

Joff gave us excellent hospitality as much as we could drink, so full of hospitality we staggered back to our diminutive Clan boats. At weekends there were three beach bums, actually four as Jeremy's mate Jerry

Price joined our merry gang striding down the beach to do battle with the waves.

I have many happy memories of our team harmlessly enjoying the good life in perfect companionship. Richard and I maudlin with drink would lurch back to the ship arm in arm tunelessly desecrating James Taylor songs, a practise we continued to this day.

Months passed and all good things came to an end, the sign on the gangplank announced our impending departure so with sad hearts we entered into a frenzy of farewell parties.

Jerry Price, me, Jeremy, Ox and Tom. Clan Ross

Waving us goodbye from the dock Richard, Tom and the faithful Kombi watched as the tugs took station and would you believe it the bloody engine wouldn't start. It used to work, perhaps we should have left it alone, the captain was not amused.

Well we had to have more farewell parties, churlish not too, and finally five days later Durban became a blur on the horizon.

At our last farewell Richard thrust a bulging suitcase in my hand to deliver back to his Mum, 'anything to declare to customs' I asked innocently, 'absolutely zippo' he replied with an angelic expression on his countenance, well he was a property developer!

Round the Cape of Good Hope and up the West Coast of Africa our crew of Durban stalwarts and newcomers steamed. Nearer and nearer beckoned the shores of old 'blighty', Europe at long last, Portuguese, Spanish and French coasts sped by as did Belgium and Holland, wait a minute we've overshot.

Our wonderful company were sending us to Germany to discharge, well I have no axe to grind with the Boche in fact in another life I worked for Bosch for twenty one years but that's another story, still, I wanted to see my Mum. In recompense they at least docked us in Hamburg so in true seamen's tradition we had a run ashore.

After visiting the museums and art galleries, not really, we headed straight for the Reeperbahn to window shop the ladies, eventually finding ourselves in the Eros centre. This place resembled a bus shelter with scantily clad ladies leaning on the rail. Not trusting ourselves after three weeks at sea our gang held hands to prevent lust taking the upper hand.

It was however too much for our South African junior, with a mighty tug he was free and disappeared into the warm embrace of one of the beauties. We waited patiently in the Eros centre snack bar for his return, these Germans think of everything! A short while later he stumped up frowning, 'like shagging a brick' he offered. Apparently everything was extra, she didn't even take her clothes off, and whilst remonstrating with her a large man appeared and our boy exited horizontally into the street.

For consolation we found a beer Keller so beloved by Germans and tourists alike. This one was typical mock Tyrolean, full of smoke, tables, wooden beams and fat Germans sitting in rows wearing lederhosen clutching foaming steins of beer. Antelope heads with complete sets of antlers hung off the walls wearing bemused expressions as if they had just charged through the plaster.

A florid complexioned accordionist led the singing accompanied by frantic stampings of feet and pounding of fists on the tables.

Amongst this mayhem wend buxom serving wenches dressed in traditional costumes with biceps like weight lifters carrying three steins of beer in each hand. Unfortunately still dazed by his early exit from the house of ill repute our South African friend decided to try his luck and pinched one of their arses and there was ample to pinch. Calmly she lowered her beer glasses and dealt him a finely timed uppercut sending him flying across the sawdust and fag end littered floor, not having a good day commented one of the boys!

Next morning enjoying a well earned Sunday lie in I was rudely awaken by a knock on my cabin door. Outside stood a delegation of Zulu's requesting a film show in their mess. Better than lying in bed I thought and organised the projector, speaker and film spools to be carried down below.

The Zulu crew only had a small drink allowance so whilst in need of a personal hair of the dog I emulated the serving wenches from the previous night and staggered into their quarters carrying two giant jugs of Tennent's draught lager. With the projector quietly humming I looked around at my audience, they seemed to be enjoying the show; well there was lots of teeth and whites of the eyes to be seen.

Talking of humming, if horses sweat, men perspire and young ladies merely glow then these lot clearly had equine tendencies. It would have made my father's day to tell you I showed them Zulu but in truth it was some dull detective story, still anything was a bonus on this grey German day.

Repairing to the bar with a long session in mind we noticed our old enemy Bank line had just docked one of their ships nearby. After fortifying ourselves with ale we put together a master plan of attack, the details getting a bit blurred as the afternoon wore on.

Basically a decoy party would storm the gangplank (walk up it) take out the duty watchman (distract him) whilst the rest of the team dressed in camouflage gear would board the ship and steal items of military importance. In fact we would wear dirty boiler suits walk up the gangplank and nick anything that wasn't bolted down.

The plan seemed feasible so to fill in time until zero hundred hours (it got dark) we took large amounts of liquid to prevent dehydration. The scene in the bar was reminiscent of John Cleese and the people's democratic Judean people's front meetings from the 'Life of Brian'! With no danger of dehydration we donned boiler suits burnt some wine corks after consuming the contents and blacked up.

What the Zulu's thought I don't know perhaps they thought we were auditioning for the black and white minstrel show!

The forward party deployed (staggered to the Bank ship) and dealt with the watchman (had a fag behind a hatch).

Silently we approached our target using the dockyard cranes as cover. (Crashing along we fell over the crane railway lines) and swarmed up the gangplank in one cohesive unit (one got lost, one had a pee and the other went home with a grazed knee). There were enough survivors fortunately to put plan B into action.

We split into two parties the first group turned their house flag and ensign upside down, then broke into the bridge and removed the ships bell, daring stuff I hear you cry. Dodging the enemy searchlights (the night watchman's torch which was as bright as a Toc H lamp) we made off with our spoils and returned triumphant to the safety of the Clan Ross bar. At the debrief (piss up) we were surprised to see the decoy party had not returned, had we causalities? Were they prisoners? Should we mount a rescue mission?

Numbed with fatigue (pissed as farts) we sadly contemplated their fate until with a loud crash they fell into the bar exhorting the praise of those great chaps of Bank line. They had been escorted to their bar and interrogated using that age old torture, forced to drink gallons of beer, then try to interpret their answers.

Next morning as the Bank line boat sailed by we saluted them loudly using their own ships bell and asked them who was in distress as their ensign was upside down, their answer was unrepeatable. I noticed that the shore party looked a bit sheepish after having enjoying their hospitality but bollocks as us soldiers says it was a brilliant mission with no casualties aside from a few sore heads.

I think I must have read one too many SAS books before writing the above tale.

We sailed on the tide, I've just finished 'Treasure Island' so watch out for 'Jim me Lads' and 'Pieces of Eight' creeping in, southwards to where the butter melts! Once more we sailed straight by England bound for rich pickings in the Med, you were warned, this trip had all the makings of a double header 'aaaahhhhaaaa shiver me timbers' whatever that means.

We passed through the straits of Gibraltar and onwards through the crystal blue waters of the Mediterranean to Marseilles. One of the officers professed to be fluid in French so after work and the usual imbibing we bundled into a taxi. Heading down town to the seedy part of the old port we eagerly awaited our interpreter's instructions to the driver for our nights sport.

Drawing a deep breath our hero with a perfect Scots Inspector Clouseau accent ordered, 'drinky drinky, womany womany jig a jig' and to give the driver his due that's what we got.

Our final destination Trieste was in sight as we lazily sailed along the Italian coast, after eight months on the Clan Ross we were finally going home. As I sadly packed my sea chests, (suitcases), I realised how much junk I had accumulated.

A surf board, ships bell, assorted nicked bits from bars and restaurants, Zulu spears and shields and of course my mate Richards belongings to be returned to his Mum. I had experienced so much on that ship, sailed with some great and not so great shipmates and seen the world or at least bits that hadn't been invaded by the package companies yet.

It was with a heavy heart we piled all our junk into taxis and took the road to the airport and home.

Homeward Bound

Falling off the plane at Heathrow I waited expectantly for my luggage to arrive. The baggage handlers were their usual efficient selves, pulling off any handles that hadn't been damaged in flight and trampling on the soft bags reducing the contents to the consistency of broken biscuits.

I managed to get my own back on the bastards. In those days luggage would rise up out of the depths then fall down a metal slide onto the travalator. A bored luggage man with a rake was supposed to make sure nothing fell off. I was waiting for my final bit of luggage when with a screech of glass fibre on metal my surfboard picked up speed and bowled the luggage man over, most satisfying.

I had to wait for him to be carried away moaning before hastily reclaiming my board and go to the intimidation hall or Customs as they are properly known. All my 'nick nacks' were worth peanuts so I approached the Gestapo with a clear conscience and had nearly escaped when a tap on the shoulder stopped me.

'Anything to declare' the officer enquired, 'absolutely nothing' I honestly replied, humming to himself he cast his eyes over my possessions and asked me to open, well I never, my mates bag. Without batting an eyelid I acquiesced, Ox had given me his word hadn't he, so after a quick rummage he stamped the bags OK and I was free.

Squeezing all my gear, the board and myself into a hire car this sailor was on the last leg back to Hockley to the family home. I couldn't wait to see Mom and Dad to give them their Zulu spears, very useful in suburban Essex I'm sure.

But first a stop in Guidea Park, to offload the much

mentioned suitcase. As usual I had a great welcome from Ma and Pa Oxley and their beautiful daughter Judy who demanded a complete run down of our adventures in the African continent. I requested a ceremonious opening of the case and to my amazement found it was full of electrical goodies. A camera, an eight-track stereo, watches, a radio, all wrapped in designer shirts, was the custom man blind?

Bidding Dick and Joan goodbye I sped down the old Southend Arterial, through Raleigh, into the top end of Hockley and finally down Bullwood Rd to the house at the end before the woods, called home.

With a fast beating heart I ran up the path and for a laugh instead of going round the back and into the kitchen I went to the front door and rapped the old knocker loudly. As the door creaked open I shouted surprise surprise, which certainly was for the two complete strangers standing there. You must be another sailor son of the last owners, they moved out two months ago.

Somewhat deflated I thanked them and drove away from my childhood home and onwards to Stone on the River Blackwater my parents new abode. This is where Dad had taught me to sail, where I had met Richard and the rest of my sailing pals and where coincidentally the love or ex love of my life spent her weekends and it was a Saturday!

Forgive me if I slip into cowboy speak, but it felt like I was going to the gunfight at the OK corral, and truthfully I was really upset.

Parking my car in the sailing Club car park I walked slowly towards the beach mentally adjusting my Stetson to shade my eyes from the hot midday Essex sun and trying to remember the words of Gary Cooper in high noon. I'm sure it wouldn't come to a shootout when I met my girl and her new fancy man but I was keeping my eyes peeled just in case they tried to head me off at the pass.

All my pals and my ex came out of the saloon, yacht club bar, they all knew how much I had loved her and how I must be hurting. Brushing them aside I walked with long strides towards her, my right hand hovering over my wallet my mouth dry and my heart pounding. She was as beautiful as ever but alas no longer mine!

I must have said hello but even after all our time together from her schooldays to just eight months ago we found we had nothing to say, it was all too late. I remember going back to meet her parents who looked awkward and I expect relieved that their daughter had escaped the 'bit' of rough from Essex'.

We met a couple of times whilst on leave and talked about old times but I was a sailor now not tied to the land, an adventurer, Essex was too small a place for me!

It was hard telling my friends about my new life, it was so far removed from any of their experiences. Mombasa brothels, night raids on ships and barking mad 'Chippies' all sound far-fetched but they had happened and somewhere in the world similar mad things are still going on, you just have to be there.

The first thing your pals say when you've been away is great to see you, where have you been? When are you going again? Your pal's wives treat you as a loose cannon because you're a single man liable to tempt the boy's back into misdeeds.

With tales to make their hair curl and the boys to wonder whether their nine to five jobs and two kids is all that's it's cracked up to be they are pleased to see you and glad when you're gone. I don't include my best pals in this they have always supported my eccentricity. I can't help it I inherited it from my folks.

After a few weeks holiday I was recalled to coast

various ships around Britain which just highlighted how much I really wanted to get away for more adventures. Unfortunately I had two more years at college to turn all the practical engineering into exam results.

Early Days

In this interlude between ship and shore I'll give you a rough guide to the Tickner family particularly my eccentric father.

I was born on the 26 March 1953 in Southend or as mother insisted we told guests, Westcliffe, more upmarket you understand! Mother thought sex was what rich people kept coal in and that a crèche is what happened when cars collide. Two brothers had preceded me, Jeremy and then Joff so by the time I arrived a little girl was first choice.

When I bawled my way into the world a deeply disappointed mother refused to speak to me and dressed me in the pink baby attire she had painstakingly knitted. Maybe that's why in later years I would at the drop of a hat don wig and gown, purely for thespian reasons of course.

Father strode off every day in his bowler and pin stripes to his job as chief clerk at Hamlet Court Rd looking for the entire world like Capt. Mainwaring of 'Dads Army' fame. We lived up a little leafy lane Brendon Way just off the infamous Southend Arterial so beloved by bikers and sports car owners who used it as a race track.

My Mom and Dad were in the iron and steel business, she ironed and he stole, not really but I had to see such a bad joke in print. We shared a beach hut with friends at Old Leigh with commanding views over the Thames mudflats. Perhaps that's where the call of the sea came from, summer afternoons watching an endless procession of ships making their way up to the still bustling port of London.

Back to the beach, the proud Tickner boys played in the mud as Mom and Dad made ham and sand sandwiches brewing endless cups of tea on a rusty

Primus stove. You can still see this fine English tradition on bank holidays when extremely old, lucky to still have a driving licence pensioners park their gleaming Ford Prefects in lay-bys. Pulling small collapsible chairs out of the boot they brew up and sup tea whilst enjoying the heady exhaust fumes of the log jammed motorists.

Before finally succumbing to senility they buy a caravan and drive at thirty mph so ensuring a clear road ahead oblivious to the ten mile tail back behind them of frustrated motorists who thought they would take the scenic route past Stonehenge thus avoiding the traffic on the motorways, haven't we all been there.

To be nearer Dad's office we moved to Bridgewater Drive, ideally situated to be next to Westcliffe High School mothers preferred seat of learning for her boys or St Thomas Moore for religious schooling seeing that Mum was a winter catholic and Dad was a Buddhist.

Fate took a hand when Dad was promoted to bank manager in the sleepy little village of Hockley twenty-five miles away. So at the tender age of five just as Buster another boy child arrived to swell the ranks we 'upsticked' and moved.

Our new home was at the end of an unmade road next to Hockley woods with a playing field at the bottom of the garden and my new primary school, a stone's throw from the house.

Not for me the transport provided for today's 'namby pamby' kids delivered in massive oversize Chelsea tractors clogging the roads around schools, a brisk walk and I was there. At the top end of our field were rusty swings and slides and a dilapidated shelter housing an ice cream and tea kiosk to quench the thirst of lovers and mothers with kids who frequented the park.

After work, the banks shut at half three in those long

ago days, Dad would take us all onto the field and teach us the finer arts of cricket. Television was banned during the summer we preferred playing outside until the swooping bats sent us hurrying home to our beds.

Father's eccentricity began to show at this time. He would arrive home from work clutching armfuls of various products and convince us they had numerous uses. One day he appeared with a ton of foam rubber. Cushions were stuffed with no regard for fire regulations, flip flop type shoes were glued together and became mandatory footwear. 'They are dual purpose' he exclaimed, 'comfortable, fits all feet sizes and in case of a spill can be used to mop up', can't argue with the logic.

As the family grew father decided to convert the house. Jeremy had gone to college appearing spasmodically on a stripped down scooter, leaving me seven, Jonathan nine and Buster two. So he split the boy's one large bedroom into two. Buster had a huge bedroom and Jonathan and I were forced to sleep in bunk beds squashed into a tiny corner of the house. I think Dad had a faulty tape measure.

Claustrophobia set in so Dad converted the playroom into a bedroom for me which due to it resemblance to a green house was stifling in the summer and freezing cold in the winter. He was a loving man and cared for his boys so his next surprise purchase was several hundred yards of assorted expanded polystyrene foam sheeting.

With this material he proceeded to cover every surface in the house including my ceiling and windows thus insulating me from the heat and cold. One downside of this was my views of the outside world were limited. Undeterred he went to the local haberdashery shop and purchased sticky backed vinyl with mountain scenes on the inside which he stuck over the foam covered windows.

There weren't many inhabitants of Hockley who could boast Swiss Mountain views from their bedrooms. Unfortunately the glue he used was suspect and one night a complete section of ceiling foam became detached and gently fell onto a severely traumatised child, who thought a ghost was attacking him. Mother curtailed his impulse buying for a while after that incident.

My bedroom doubled as a classroom twice a week when mother ran a play school, she had seven kids to entertain. When they got too rowdy she would drag them round Hockley woods for a walk accompanied by our ginger cat mewing forlornly. Shanty, the family Corgi, was too old and knackered for any exercise like walking.

Our house like most houses of that era had no central heating, relying on gas or electric bar fires in the downstairs rooms and natural convection upwards to heat the bedrooms. Guests would beat the doors down to get outside, it was warmer there.

We boys relied on feline hot water bottles, ginger and white cat, very imaginatively named I know, to warm our beds. An hour before bedtime they would be coaxed into our arms and shoved under the blankets. By the time you had undressed before frostbite attacked your vital parts the bed or one cat-sized bit would be warm.

You had to make the most of it, as the elder two boys at their appointed bedtime would pull your blankets back and seize the confused creatures for their turn. I perfected this art by using a larger version, my kid brother Buster!

Father eventually relented on the heating front and one day some electrical men came and installed some big steel boxes, which they filled with bricks. The theory behind these monstrosities was they would heat up at night using cheap electricity and give off the heat during the day. So much for the theory, they actually became luke warm by dawn and rapidly turned to blocks of ice during the day.

Once again father capitulated due to the sight of his family wearing duffel coats at the dinner table and the difficulty of using knives and forks wearing woollen mittens. The charge times were adjusted and for a few weeks we lived in heated luxury until mother realised the boxes made ideal clothes dryers. She turned the whole house into a giant Turkish bath with people appearing and disappearing through the steam as they made their tentative way around the building.

I blame my parents for my piles, the warm boxes made quite comfortable seats when the mounds of still damp but beautifully steamed clothes were removed. Talking of clothes, Mother had been a governess to a wealthy family at one stage who still remembered to send a trunk each year full of clothes that their family had outgrown. Unfortunately the two families kids ages did not match consequently we were dressed in high quality clothing which never fitted.

I went to school dressed as a Roman centurion and Joff as a Japanese Admiral. Actually poor Joff got the raw deal he wore a pair of outsize blue corduroy shorts right through to the second year of senior school while all his mates wore drainpipe trousers. During the summer we would never take our blazers off as mother had shortened our shirtsleeves by putting huge tucks in them.

I remember taking 'O' levels with the sun beating through the schools huge glass windows with sweat pouring off me but couldn't take the jacket off because I was too embarrassed, how stupid was I?

Mom and Dad believed in functional clothing not

style. Whilst all my mates wore winkle picker shoes Dad went out and bought me a pair of *'Start Rite'* shoes the ones with soles covered in animal tracks with a compass in the heels. Very useful in the Yukon maybe but in Essex I would suggest of minimal benefit.

I saved up my pocket money sixpence a week and eventually purchased a sharp pair of winkle pickers. Each morning I would get to the bus stop early thus avoiding comment from my pals on my *'Start Rites'*. I'd change into the pickers hidden in a box behind the shelter, conceal the offending pair and there I stood, a real cool dude or swinger or whatever the then current name for a schoolboy with pointed feet was.

'Levi' jeans were all the range then and probably still are. You had to buy a pair a size too large, lie in a cold bath wearing them until they achieved that shrunk worn out look that was the fashion. The fact you would contract pneumonia or at least a bad head cold and had dyed blue legs showed what a martyr to fashion you were.

After months of pleading for a pair of *'Levi'* jeans Dad sent me to Millets to buy a pair of cheap denims, can you imagine the disgrace, so I bought some *Levi's* and told Dad Millets had sold out. With a promise to thrash me alive if I was telling lies he rang Millets and thank God they actually had sold out so up to the bathroom I went with a very relieved spring in my step. My pocket money couldn't run to a button down *Ben Sherman* shirt but Mom had knitted me a snazzy red Arran jumper to complete my outfit. I cut quite a dash with my *Levi's,* winkle pickers and red jumper in the sailing club bar despite the fact that mum had knitted about twenty of these damn woollies for most of the other members.

Jeremy and Joff on Joff's Lambretta

Jeremy's trips back home from college in Southampton bear a mention, this was long before the M3 and M25, it was a tortuous route taking at least five hours. His mode of transport didn't help. It was once a *Lambretta* scooter complete with side panels, footrests, kick-starter and the like.

After numerous fallings off the bike was just a bare frame with wheels, engine and fuel tank taped on.

The throttle cable once attached to a twist grip would be wound round his hand as he battled through the winter snow and ice. We would have to lift him off the wreck on his arrival and slowly thaw him out on one of those bloody steel boxes. Finally he bit the bullet and purchased some sort of old Ford, max speed forty-mph. One night on the Winchester bypass he saw an E type Jag in his wing mirror.

A fit of madness overcame him as he decided to race it. At fifty five mph the tiny engine gave a despairing bang and bits flew all over the road. He managed to salvage one piston with a bent shaft, which he later mounted on a wooden plaque entitled 'Piston Broke'. It was a comment on the financial and drunken state of most students.

Joff had a more upmarket, well more complete bike, a 225cc *Lambretta GT* bored out to 250cc, boy did it go! You had to wear all the kit, parker jacket, twenty mirrors and loads of foxtails hanging off aerials.

Joff used to work on it in the side alley, finely adjusting the carburettor with a large hammer and some new and very imaginative swear words.

Round the back of the house Dad with a job lot of timber had built an entrance shed into the back door complete with loads of glass and Perspex. It housed along with all our welly boots and various cat and dog bowls a farting washing machine. Without fail on the final turn of the drum on its spin cycle it would emit a perfect fart much to the amusement of us small boys.

Keep the Home Fires Burning

My parents believed in separate holidays, separate from the children that is, they would farm us out to unsuspecting pretend aunts whilst they disappeared to the sun, we loved it. One year they thought we should stay at home and get Mrs Hedges our charlady to move in for two weeks. We also loved that as Mrs Hedges came from the school of cooking that included chips with everything, there were always large vats of boiling oil bubbling away.

I won't say she was an arsonist but she did a damn good impression of one. The first fire set the clothes hanger alight, one of those ones you pulled up to the ceiling on pulleys and ropes. We escaped through the front door as neighbours doused the flames. The second was much more satisfactory with the whole kitchen on fire filling the house with acrid foam rubber and polystyrene-fuelled smoke.

We used the drainpipe on the side of the house that time and had to be housed at the headmaster's house. At least we were safe with him, as he preferred little girls! Chastened by this experience, Mom and Dad bought a caravan and found an empty site on the Blackwater estuary which became our weekend haunt and eventually their home.

When mother's wrath had subsided, Dad bought the kit boat glued it together in the back garden and the rest is history, all the family and eventually their kids became sailors. So during the summers we would load the old Morris Traveller with kids, cats and food and disappear to the caravan to swim, sail and explore the marshes and beaches.

The long summer holidays were best playing outside until ten, dodging bats and making expeditions to far off islands. It was a cross between the Famous

Five and Swallows and Amazons all played out on muddy Essex river banks, who needed foreign holidays?

Virgin Sailors

I had tired of dads *Yachting World Pram* in which kid brother Buster and I spent many happy hours pottering a few hundred yards from the shore and aspired to greater things like racing a *Cadet* up at Stone sailing club. There were two benefits for this move, one the boats were faster and didn't resemble prams, and two I was starting to become aware of the opposite sex and the club boasted a cadet section with loads of girlies.

Before Dad would let me move on he bought an *Enterprise*, this was a blue sailed fourteen footer with inflatable buoyancy bags in case he capsized. As he spent most of the time upside down the bags were a good investment. True to form he appeared one day with a clutch of misshapen soggy objects he had found in a boat sale. 'They are the latest things in life jackets' he explained pulling them over our heads. They were filled with Kapok lined with an abrasive material which rubbed the skin off your neck, we used to boast the chafe marks were love bites. Dad won many races with this boat with us as crew and yes it did prepare me for the rough and tumble of cadet racing. The best adventure with the *Enterprise* came not on the water but on her trailer on the way to an open meeting just up the road. Dad decided he couldn't be bothered to de-rig the boat, take the mast and boom off, but would tow it up the road all standing. We hadn't even left the caravan park when the wire shrouds holding the mast up met some overhead high tension wires. With a loud bang and a puff of smoke the *Enterprise* became a rowing boat, 'don't tell your mother' was his rueful comment.

So up the road I went and got a job crewing for Sue in *Cadet* 3180 an immaculate piece of marine furniture tended by Alf her devoted dad. She was good, I learnt fast and we won loads of races travelling all over the country competing in open meetings. We came third in the *Cadet* nationals in Plymouth with Sue taking the top girl's helmswoman's position, at the prize giving we were presented with the Mermaid trophy by the Town Mayor.

In anticipation of this glory Mom and Dad had furnished a prize giving outfit from the hand me down chest. I have the press photo still as evidence against the style council and inhumanity to small children. I wore a hairy *Harris Tweed* jacket three sizes too big, well at least it hid the shirt sleeves, ankle length trousers, mom got my leg measurements wrong, those bloody *Start Rite* shoes and topping the whole ensemble I sported one of my Mothers infamous haircuts. No hair at the back and a sort of diagonal fringe, fine for the new age era but an absolute 'no no' in the 60's.

My pal Bob who had a caravan on our site joined Stone sailing club and we soon were racing every weekend against a competitive fleet of boys and girls. By this time I had flunked my eleven plus and was spending three hours a day on buses going back and forth to St Thomas Moore in sunny Southend.

It was boys only so the only access I had to girls was through sailing, they were different from the ones on the bus who sent me stammering and blushing every time they deigned to talk to me.

In the summer of my eleventh year just before cadet week there was a knock on our caravan door where the Cadet Captain and a good looking boy stood. 'Good evening Mrs Tickner this is Richard Oxley, he's racing this week and staying in his parents caravan opposite, do you mind looking after him'?

This was the beginning of a friendship that spanned thirty-eight years and many continents, which ended in the spring of this year when he passed away after fighting cancer for five years. But boy did we live life in the fast lane, I cannot recall one idea that we didn't seize upon, give it a good shaking and pushed it to the limit.

I persuaded Mom and Dad to let me hitch to Stone every Friday night as they either drove down Saturday afternoon or Sunday morning wasting in my view valuable sailing time, later to become drinking time. So if you ever picked up a small boy, not in the biblical sense, between Rettingdon Turnpike and Stone, many belated thanks.

An older boy, Steve Boulton joined our gang, whose Dad owned a twenty foot open sailing boat called Folly. With this ship we could venture even further, to Osea Island or Maldon a pretty town at the head of the River Blackwater filled with old Thames barges.

These were halcyon day's boys and girls crammed together on the good ship Folly, waves washing over us and the sun always shone. The girls often wore bikinis, which they were beginning to fill quite generously, unfortunately no matter how hard or often we pulled our genitalia the girls were developing faster.

Mr and Mrs Boulton were diamonds, generous to a fault they would do anything for their son Steven and his friends. This often involved moving out to let us hold wild parties in their cottage at Stone. Wild as you can get with four pint tins of *Watneys Red Barrel* which defeated most attempts to open until stabbed in desperation with a screwdriver and spraying the contents all over the room. It was after one such incident that Steve's father, a master builder by trade redecorated the cottage with advice from us.

Lime green walls with bright orange curtains was the end result, come on it was the seventies man, psychedelic rules! 'Lucy in the sky with diamonds'.

Watneys Red Barrel takes me back to Hockley where me and my mate Morris Barnes a son of the local coal merchant were playing on the rusty roof of the old shelter at the top our field. Actually we were hiding from irate lovers. We used to creep up on semi clad couples in shady secluded copses in the woods, wait until a hairy arse would get up to full speed then throw stones at it escaping on our push bikes, simple pleasures as I recall.

The tin roof was ninety percent rust, which was no match for two teenager's weight as we fell through into a musty storeroom. Imagine our delight when we found a case of *Babycham* and two of those giant vats of *Bulmer* cider lying there. Under the cover of night we removed them and wheeled our spoils on our bike crossbars down to the coal yard where after a prolonged sampling we hid them.

Monday night was Scout night, it also became drinks night. British Bulldog played in a dusty village hall, us full of cider bouncing off walls was a sight to see. Poor old Akela thought we were full of high spirits and she was right. Morris and I would keel over right in the middle of dyb, dyb dyb and sodding dob dob dob and as for ging gang gooly gooly! (Dyb scout talk for do your best, Dob do our best, I have no idea what ging gang gooly means)

One night we had to go on a night march through Hockley woods to Southend. Morris and I fortified with the last of the cider and carrying the remnants of the *Babycham* staggered along behind. The scout leader stopped and stood there in the dark. 'boys' he whispered, 'sniff deeply you can smell the fumes from Southend brewery', the prat was lost it was me and Morris standing upwind.

Academia was not my strongest point, Mom and Dad tried their best but all I wanted to do was sail and to be brutally honest to get past number three with Sue one of the more developed girl cadets. Mom sent me to piano lessons with a lovely old piano teacher who lived half way down our road, which was the only good bit, at least she was local. I got to grade seven and to everyone's surprise won my age groups top prize in the Southend music competition. I can still play the Chopin piece after all this time. My dear parents listened to my moans about classical music and found me a jazz teacher but I was too far gone with the sailing bug and bunked off every lesson, I have always regretted not sticking with the old 'Joanna'!

So weekends became sailing and parties, Richards's caravan or Steve's parent's cottage the chosen venues. Unfortunately no matter how much we boasted and lied to each other we still hadn't done it, gone all the way, had our evil way, for fucks sake fifteen and still virgins, the shame!

Some girls were on the pill but they were rare so we had to get condoms, but who looked old enough? And where did you get them? My Mom butchered my hair so I had no access to barbers and their famous line 'something for the weekend sir' Men's magazines advertised Durex, buy in complete confidence supplied in brown paper packaging but they supplied only by the gross. One hundred and forty four, that would last at our present rate of usage i.e. nil, a lifetime.

Steve by now had a Suzuki 50 cc moped whilst we at one year younger still had pushbikes. There was a little pub in Tillingham eight miles away run by a very old lady who would serve us drinks. On a Friday night, if you were lucky, you could see the strange sight of Steve on his Suzuki towing five of us on bikes around the country lanes joined by a long rope.

Well the going was fine but coming back fortified by as many beers as our pocket money would allow was carnage with ditches and bushes and many other prominent land marks leaving their marks on us. One dark night I drove the Suzuki back pissed still wearing sunglasses, I still have the scar where I missed a bend! God knows what happened to my mates hanging on grimly behind.

We boys decided in the summer of our fifteenth year that the matter of our virginity had to be addressed. Steve was now seventeen with his driving licence and a Renault 4, the car where the gear stick, shaped like an umbrella handle, stuck out of the dash board.

One of his mates a Jewish chap with a fondness for bacon sent off for a gross of Durex. Unfortunately his grandmother caught him trying one on for size but he explained they were a new type of party balloon with a special bit for catching spit at the end. How he explained what it was doing on his dick we never found out!

Steve, Ashley, Bob, Richard and I complete with tent, gross of Durex and high expectations drove down to the sunny beaches of Polzeath in Cornwall. We had a great holiday, learnt how to surf, stroked some breasts and returned virginity and the box of Durex intact.

Winter was upon us, no more sailing but at least we had Steve's Xmas party to look forward to, held at his parent's mansion in Totteridge and Whetstone North London. I had met a new girl in the sailing club who showed great promise, I had undone her bra strap!

As a preamble to the big party the Cadet Captain held a smaller affair in Chelmsford. I waited in vain for my date who failed to materialise so in the way of these parties I found a bottle of Crabbies Green ginger wine in the kitchen and drank it. The last place I was sick was in the garden which is where they found me covered in frost and vomit. Steve and Richard took me back to the caravan site leaving me with my head down the chemical loo disposal pit. Ox mistakenly tried to make me drink a gallon of coffee which is why to this day I never drink coffee and I can't say I'm too fond of green ginger wine either.

Steve's party loomed. Big Dave another much older and fatter friend picked us up in his Humber Snipe, he needed big cars due to his size and delivered us to the venue!

Steve's parents had been sent away for the weekend but had fortunately shored up the party floor with acrow props mindful of the exuberant dancing of previous years.

Poor old granny, who lived downstairs had to watch television surrounded by steel reinforcements, fortunately she was stone deaf so she missed the Beach Boys and us singing 'Good Vibrations' at the top of our voices.

A young lady, who will remain nameless took me upstairs and had her evil way in the quietness of a hidden bedroom. Unfortunately not hidden enough as Ox who shared everything I did burst in and pulled the sheets off the bed. 'You bastard' I roared and being the perfect gentleman excused myself from the post coital cuddle and ran after him straight into the middle of the crowded dance floor. Seeing as I was only wearing a used condom on a rapidly shrinking willy I beat a hasty retreat back to the arms or rather chilly back of my loved one. The deed was done!

Big Dave feeling tired and confused decided to drive back at four a.m. but an oak tree had uprooted itself and moved into the middle of the great North road which slightly impeded his progress so he returned very bloody but unbowed. We all voted the party a tremendous success including granny whose ceiling had survived the onslaught for another year.

Whilst In Steve party mode I must tell you what happened at the next Christmas party. Steve's parents refused to abandon house so they were banned to the furthest bedroom of the mansion known only to some and reached up a tortuous staircase.

Ashley, he of the condoms, was one of the few in the know, and to his surprise had pulled. Full of lust and the odd gallon of beer he found his way through the labyrinth of passages and staircases much like a Harry Potter adventure, to the door of the bedroom.

Years later when Steve's parents became Fred and Dotty to us they told us their side of the story.

They were tucked up in bed reading quietly by the light of a ceiling lamp when they heard the furtive whisperings of Ashley and his prey. Pulling the light cord they shrank into the corner of the bed and waited. Suddenly the door swung open revealing the lovers. Not wasting time on niceties, Ashley pulled off all his clothes and in a dramatic gesture swept the blankets and duvet off the bed. Jumping onto the bed he lay legs akimbo exhorting the girl to join him.

Fred calmly pulled the light cord revealing Dotty with the remaining sheet pulled tight to her chin and the naked Ashley sporting a rapidly shrinking erection. 'Good evening Ashley' he commented wryly, the girl won the hundred yard dash and Ashley the high jump as he fled the room, the house and probably the country.

Fred and Dotty were to feature in many of our adventures as they sort of adopted me. My final destination of my youthful hitching became their cottage where there was always a warm welcome and a hot dinner. Sadly they have both passed on but I will never forget their kindness and unfailing sense of humour.

They were invaded every weekend by hordes of

cadets who drank them dry and used all their facilities. Stone had no mains drainage so each house had a cesspit, which had to be emptied periodically. On one occasion as the tanker was sucking away, Fred, his builder's curiosity aroused as the pipe kept jamming, peeped down into the pit.

'How unusual' he commented 'I wonder how they got there, your mother and I certainly don't use them anymore'. The top of the surface was full of condoms, 'enough rubber to keep a formula one team equipped with tyres for a year' he suggested. Get out of that I thought?

The summer holidays were our happiest time but also became a bit of a drag mid week. Stone boasted one pub frequented by the stink pot brigade, East Enders with Jags and powerboats. The sailing club where we sailed our dinghies only opened at weekends.

Now we were mobile with Steve's car, the opportunities should have been endless but apathy had set in until a chance overhearing of a parental conversation stirred our loins into action. Freddy and Dotty and some social worker friends were talking early one afternoon in August about a new council initiative. A sailing school for underprivileged girls from the East end of London had been set up in Heybridge basin only twenty five miles from Stone.

Apparently, they continued, the girls were taught how to sail during the day and were allowed out for a couple of hours a night before being banged up in a dormitory. The engine was already revving and doors banging behind us as Steve, Ashley and I heard the sentence end. Allowed out, yahoo. We bumped into another friend Paul in his snazzy open top three wheeler as he came out of Maylandsea, so we explained our mission. He joined the hunt as we roared along the winding country lanes through Maldon and on to Heybridge. The one tiny road in peters out at a canal lock leading to Chelmsford overlooked by the Jolly Sailor and the Old Ship public houses.

Screeching to a dusty halt we sloped into the pub wondering how we would recognise the girls. We shouldn't have worried. Amongst the smock wearing, pipe smoking bargees and the local domino players, two dyed blonde stunners in tight skirts and low blouses leaving nothing for the imagination, stood out like pork chops at a Jewish wedding.

Before we could summon up courage they spotted us and teetered over on their stilettos, 'buy us drink boys' they rasped through tobacco sodden lungs. I was quickest on the draw and paid the penalty of two double gin and tonics, with cherries and umbrellas! Leading us outside to perch on the lock wall we admired their panties as they told us how bored they were and asked 'where was the action'.

Moving quickly in for the kill we told them about the bars in Stone and the all night drinking club, my parent's caravan actually but that's too much detail! Come over tomorrow they said and we'll party all night and break back into the dormitory in the morning, no problem and be prepared.

What the fuck did that mean, be prepared, how did they know I was still a Boy Scout or could they possibly mean be protected, did Ashley still have those one hundred and forty three Durex left! One small hitch there was four boys and only the two of them.

'Can you find two more girls'? 'We'll try' they shouted back as they clambered over a fence leaving us with one final view of panties and four erections. Punching the air we planned to meet Paul at the bottom of the road at eight the following night and drove the long road back full of anticipation.

Freddy and Dotty were more than a little bit

suspicious when booted and suited Ashley, Steven and I told them 'don't wait up as we could be late'. I forgot to tell you that Steve was a bit of a Mummy's boy and that she always waited up for him and if she knew we were meeting two slappers from the East End she would have a blue fit.

We roared pass Paul's road a full half hour early hoping to reduce the odds, and saw him just ahead obviously with the same idea, all's fair in love and lust we reasoned. Standing outside the Jolly Sailor were the girls in shorter, tighter gear but still only two. 'We couldn't get any other fuckers to come' they explained politely, 'no problem' we answered through gritted teeth.

The small one grabbed hold of Steve's arm, he obviously must be rich to own a car and jumped in the front. The odds were three to one now. Paul leering in anticipation swung open the door to his sporty three wheeler and said to the more buxom girl, 'hop in I'll take you for a spin'. 'I'm not getting in that fucking wheelbarrow' she replied, two to one.

Playing his master stroke Ashley made his move. Opening the back door he motioned for the girl to get in, ready for the follow up slide with the arm along the back rest, soon to drop on her protesting shoulder. Fortunately she was too cute for that, 'after you' she murmured huskily, Ashley jumped in a smile on his face which turned into a snarl as grasping my hand she bundled me in next and practically sitting on my crutch slid on board slamming the door behind her.

Heavy petting I believe was the sixties version of what happened on the journey to Stone. Ashley was ejected outside Steve's parent's cottage with threats not to blow the gaffe ringing in his ear. 'Sod the bar' the girls said 'where's the drinks and beds'. Steve's foot nearly went through the floor as we roared back to my caravan. In anticipation we had stashed some hooch there earlier, 'undo me' ordered my companion so with trembling hands I obliged and was ogling her splendour whilst tugging the double bed out of the wall.

I could hear through the partition Steve was at a similar stage when a car went by loudly bibbing its horn. Even worse we heard Dotty's voice shouting, 'I know you're in there you swine's, and with two strumpets', remarkably well informed I thought as I chose to ignore her and got on with the task in hand.

Now it's very difficult to fornicate with your mate's mother going round and round your caravan like Red Indians attacking a wagon train. Finally Steve's nerve cracked, 'we'll have to make a run for it' he informed the bemused not to say frustrated threesome. Waiting for a pause in the attack we sprinted for the car and with a crash of gears we escaped.

All was not lost as we did pause for a while in a lay by, so aptly named I mused after we dropped the girls off. By this time it was two am. It seemed we had been driving for hours back and forward along these bloody country lanes and here is the twist the Renault only has a small fuel tank.

Just outside of the village of Steeple the engine coughed and pulled to a halt. Fucking marvellous I thought now we have to walk home. An hour later as we trudged along I saw some familiar headlights. The car pulled up revealing Dotty driving in a dressing gown with Fred in his pyjamas in the passenger seat. In the back seat looking smug sat the traitor Ashley. 'Run out of fuel I suppose' said Dotty distinctly frosty, so back to the abandoned car we drove where Fred got out a petrol can and proceeded to refuel the old Renault ready to follow us home.

Dotty turned her car around and with not another word drove us back to Stone. Even in her anger she made us tea and biscuits. An hour went by and still no sign of Fred so off we went all the way back to find him standing next to the locked car clutching the empty petrol can half frozen. 'You drove off with the keys' he said through chattering teeth.

They closed the Heybridge club soon after and nine months later there were two extra mouths to feed in the East end, the girls must have been quite liberal with their affections!

Dad by this time had moved up in the boating world, leaving dinghies, he bought a *Silhouette* the smallest cabin cruiser in the world. This was rapidly replaced with a nineteen foot yacht a *Seamew*, lifting keel and four berths, luxury. Dad, Mum a chart and myself went up the East coast for a holiday. The chart flew overboard after just an hour so navigating was interesting especially as Dad's eyesight is not perfect!

West Mersea, Brightlingsea, Harwich, this was deep-sea stuff, all of thirty miles in three days. Up the Orwell we ventured, a pretty Suffolk river with trees sweeping down to the riverbanks. Pin Mill was our goal, home of old Thames barges and dilapidated house boats. The Butt and Oyster was the mecca for 'bargees' and fellow 'yachties' where we spent a most convivial evening.

I think it was the first time I had a drink in a pub with my folks, usually me and the 'bruv's' were left outside in the car with four lemonades and a packet of crisps. As ever the tide had gone out leaving Dad to pull the dinghy with Mum and I in it through two hundred yards of stinking mud before rowing unsteadily out to the boat. Dad checked the anchor and pronouncing it safe we all turned in for the night with the promise of an early start for the return trip.

A loud hail awoke us at five am. Scrambling up on deck we saw a different view from the night before. In fact we were in the middle of Harwich harbour having dragged our anchor through all the moorings and several bends in the river, quite a feat of navigation for an unmanned boat. The hail came from a passing tug that had narrowly missed cutting us in two. Acknowledging his frantic fist waving, father exclaimed 'that's saved us a couple of hours, hoist the sails and set course for home'.

A year later my pal Richard and I borrowed the boat for the same trip and got thrown out of most of the pubs as we were only sixteen with just a scrap of bum fluff on our chins trying to compete with the 'bargees' full on beards.

Dinghy Days

The Blackwater is arguably the best dinghy sailing river on the East coast, wide enough to set good races, a strong tide to test your nerves beating up the shore in a few inches of water and some good bars to brag in after.

Besides Stone there was a sailing school at Bradwell, which lay in the shadow of a huge nuclear power station. With all that electricity being generated on our doorstep we often wondered at the high frequency of local power cuts, perhaps the power station man in charge of fuses owned a local candle and torch shop?

Further up the river were Marconi, Maylandsea Bay and several other yacht clubs all the way up to Maldon. On a Sunday the whole river was full of brightly coloured dinghy sails, sailors enjoying their day off from the drudgery of work. Years ago sailing garb consisted of a mixture of other sportswear, hockey shorts, tennis shirts, rugby sweaters, and running shoes or in wet weather, garden boots!

Fashion and modern materials were invented enabling normally sane and sombre suit clad businessmen to don loud skin tight wet suits complete with racy logos like wet and wild. The same thing happened to cycling, driving along a country road you might find a swarm of fat men perched on tiny saddled push bikes. Flicking through a myriad of gears they wore obscenely tight Lycra shorts, multi -striped and logoed tops with some sort of ribbed bone dome strapped to their head.

Actually they seem to have a great time in the pretence of getting fit. One veteran cyclist admitted they started the morning by peddling to a café for a fry up then proceeded to spend the rest of the day perambulating between pubs before wobbling home pissed but well exercised.

Most sailing clubs held regattas inviting sailors from all the other clubs. A poster would appear on your notice board with sailing details but more importantly the social arrangements. Richard and I one weekend noted that Marconi were holding a bash and here's the clincher, dance and drink until dawn with Maldon's number one disco it loudly proclaimed.

That's for us we said and went down to polish the bottom of his dinghy a *Scorpion* by name, fast and macho, sort of like how we regarded ourselves. The next weekend saw us planing about the river off Marconi in a fresh breeze, the spray blowing away the remnants of the previous night's excesses helping us to win in a competitive class of similarly hung over sailors.

That evening after stuffing down what purported to be beef burgers at the mandatory BBQ we made our way up to the bar to survey the talent along with all the other guys. Female sailors were in the minority so you had to be quick. Richard spotted Diane a popular Stone girl, popular because of her habit of dispensing hand jobs in Richards's caravan at weekends. This accounted for the queue of lads outside his van on Saturday afternoons all smoking and yarning.

Talking with Diane with her back to me was a dark haired girl we did not recognise. Walking over we discussed the game plan, I'll take Diane and you try the new one said Richard. 'Hi girls', the good-looking bastard rejoined, 'fancy a drink'.

The stranger turned to face me and I turned to mush, she was beautiful and what a figure, 'whelps youse nom' I stuttered turning bright red, get a grip on yourself you prat I thought. 'Wendy' the vision replied. After a faltering start we drank and danced the night away as promised by Maldon's number one disco who were truly atrocious.

Richard and I discussed tactics whilst peeing away some of the gallons of beer we had consumed. He had just come back from a holiday in Majorca where he discovered champagne and Spanish fly! 'Look at this' he said pulling out of his pocket a little round tin with tiny Spanish writing on it. Not speaking Spanish we thought it said, dip your dickio in the ointio, 'what does it do' I asked. Apparently it had aphrodisiac properties that made your willy double in size and allowed you to shag all night. All that in such a little tin I thought.

Alcohol induced braveness or stupidity forced us to experiment. I liberally smeared my offending member with what felt like Dubbin, not that I had ever put Dubbin on my willy you understand. Richard was more cautious with his application.

Back to the dancing, we were mid 'Oh Maggie I wished I'd never seen your face', when our willies burst into flames. Rushing back to the loo we plunged our dicks into the sink spinning the cold tap on, steam billowed up from the conflagration. At that moment Marconi's commodore strode in for a comfort break, 'lads don't piss in the sink there is a urinal free' he pointed out. For once in our lives we were speechless, well what could we say.

In the back of Richards Austin 1100 on the way home Wendy and I indulged in some modest activity then we bade the girls a chaste goodnight. 'Thank you for respecting me, whispered Wendy as she promised to see me again. The fact that the only thing I wanted to put my willy in at that moment was a fridge I kept to myself.

Now I don't want you to think Richards's caravan was solely used for carnal activity we did kip there sometimes and mostly on our own. Going to clean the van however became a pseudonym for horizontal activity.

Steve had met a great girl called MR who besides looking fab often sailed the pants off us. One day the loving couple were in need of some privacy so asked Richard if they could 'clean the van'. We decamped to Bob's house to watch the rugby.

Now Steve liked his creature comforts and as it was September the caravan was a bit chilly. Trying to light the oil fire he discovered it was empty but with a stroke of inspiration remembered a fuel can under the van.

Shortly afterwards there was a knock on Bobs door revealing something out of a Tom and Jerry cartoon where a firework had exploded in the cats face. Steve stood there covered in soot, no eyebrows, singed hair and a rather shocked expression on his face. 'I've blown the bloody caravan up' he said, not comforted at all by the sight of us rolling about on the floor in fits of laughter. 'How' asked Richard, 'well I filled the stove up with the paraffin in the spare jerry can and when I put a match to it boom, MR is not best pleased I can tell you'.

'Seeing as the spare can was full of petrol for the mower I'm not surprised' commented Richard as we went to survey the scene. The van was still standing but completely covered in soot with bits of curtain flapping in the breeze torn apart by the explosion.

We had three days to clean the place up before Richards's parents were due. Applying the last coat of paint as they arrived I added explosions to the list of effective contraception, along with excessive alcohol and mothers driving around caravans.

My ongoing relationship with the love of my life ie the agricultural machinery daughter, you remember, the chronology of this missive may make you think I was a bit of a Casanova but I was in the most part monogamous not to say monotonous, was slightly thwarted by her parents attempts to hide her away. Seeing that she was at boarding school in Suffolk they were in the main successful but she was available during holidays.

I had passed my driving test by now so was mobile when Mom lent me her battered Citroen. On one glorious occasion Big Dave offered his five litre Dodge left hand drive push button geared monstrosity for the night. As I entered her parents gravel drive I gunned the engine spraying his measly Rover 3.5 litre with pebbles, very satisfying. We couldn't go far as it ate the fuel and wouldn't fit up most roads in the area but the bench seat made an admirable bed.

Passing my test had been an ordeal seeing as Jeremy and my Dad were my instructors. Driving up Maldon hill, the steepest in the area, in brother's vintage Morris Minor with hand painted L signs fore and aft Jeremy applied the hand brake. With a cough of protest the engine stalled leaving me and a trail of other motorist stuck halfway up the near vertical slope. The clutch was on its last legs whilst the handbrake was usually supplemented by a house brick under the back wheel.

With a clash of gears and some smoke from the clutch we moved victoriously backwards causing some consternation from my fellow motorists before leapfrogging up the hill. At the third attempt I passed my test and celebrated that evening by missing a bend and putting the car in a ditch. My passengers full of local ale lifted her out so we could clank our way back. I had bent a front wheel but 'Dashes' the local scrap yard supplied a replacement, not the same size but hey it was round, the road holding was a bit indifferent however.

Putting aside their natural aversion to the 'bit of rough from Hockley' I was invited to join the girlfriend's family for a slap up meal in one of Essex's top restaurants, the *Moat House* in Brentwood.

Borrowing a brothers suit which fitted where it touched we sallied forth in the company 'roller'. Aperitif enquired the waiter, 'pint of bitter please' I said which stood out a bit amongst the gin and tonics. Deciding to keep a lower profile with the food I ordered the same dishes as the rest not knowing what the hell they were.

I had never eaten in a posh restaurant before let alone one of Henry the Eight's hunting lodges. A small dish with something on it arrived with delicate slivers of brown bread and a lemon, what the fuck was this I thought and what's this funny shaped knife. Taking a huge bite I ended up with a mouthful of fish bones. 'You like mackerel' kindly enquired the Mother, nodding my agreement I choked silently to death before realising one should remove the offensive items behind a discreetly positioned napkin.

One course down, still alive but what was Chateau Briand and why did we want it blue. So its steak that's more like it as I bit into a large slice, what the fuck it's not cooked, what type of chef have they got here. Just before I summoned the waiter to tell him they had forgotten to light the stove the father said, 'good to see you like rare meat so many youngsters ruin their steaks having them well done'.

This particular youngster wanted his cremated I can tell you and for years after had well done steaks and never ate fish again.

As Tolkien might have said all that happened long ago in a land far far away, I've just reread Lord of the Rings and decided it's just made up words with a very very long story strung around them, compulsive reading though.

Back to work

The long summer came to an end and Southampton college beckoned but at least this time I was a hairy arsed son of the sea with a few miles under my belt and a good line in stories to regale motorists when hitching. Wendy and I were now an item and I had found new accommodation with Jeremy's godmother Jose living on a farm in Hedge End. The brown-coated instructors were now friends saving all their venom for the gob shite first years with their shiny new uniforms and school satchels. Life resettled into pub-crawls and all those other pranks that students play with limited funds.

My hitching career resumed with a new destination Wendy's house until I finally scraped enough money together to buy a Triumph Herald, one careful owner, never raced or rallied seventy-five quid and it was mine. We had two years of college before taking our second engineer tickets, a lifetime away it seemed.

Sailing on the East Coast continued but having tired of spending each weekend with our arses dangling in the water on dinghies we moved up into cruisers. Richard bought a 1920's canoe sterned twenty-four footer named Stealaway in which we cruised the rivers of East Anglia.

Ox then had the bright idea to sail to Holland and cruise their inland waterways, which was a major trip for us boys.

With meticulous planning we provisioned, even taking some food to go with the crates of beer. Stealaway was propelled by a *Stewart Turner* petrol engine which belonged in a museum, electrical power was supplied by a dynamo purchased from our old friend Dashes the scrap merchant. We now sail to Holland in a few hours on fast racing boats. Stealaway took four days, drifting up and down the Dutch, French and Belgium coasts. Ray, Big Dave's brother was very seasick, for the first day frightened he was going to die, over the next two days frightened he wasn't! Finally we made Ostend the town that never sleeps with discos and sleazy bars that stayed open all night serving Euro piss as the local beer was known.

Nursing the engine and four sore heads we sailed to Flushing and motored up the Middleburg canal. The Dutch have several good things going for them, they are unfailingly courteous and kind to fellow sailors. They also have fabulous inland sailing waters and a special kind of green paint which glows from all their doors and shutters. Due to most of their land being reclaimed, thus flat, cycling is a national pastime, however the skiing is crap!

We cruised around Middleburg, Veere, Goes and Zierikzee finally popping back into the North Sea at Rotterdam after negotiating their massive locks. The Stewart Turner engine had its fun too, it either ticked along at one knot or burst into full speed when not required. We were quietly gliding alongside an immaculate Dutch yacht tied up inside a lock, the family enjoying a fine lunch in their cockpit with Bob poised on our foredeck to step lightly onto their deck to make fast. Our engine sensing the occasion burst into life causing Bob to jump straight onto their table throwing their lunch and drinks into the air before being dragged along their deck vainly trying to stop our boat from hitting the lock gates. The bloody engine sulked after that incident and refused to start. Fortunately the lovely Dutch family mollified with a couple of pints of our English beer towed us out of the lock and waved us on our way.

There is a much told story about an old boy that cruised the Dutch waterways for many years and the friends he made in ports along the way, which bears another airing. This chap and his beautiful wooden boat made an annual pilgrimage across the North Sea to sail in the inland seas of Holland. Over the years his Dutch friends would join him in a convivial glass or two sitting in his cockpit.

Time creeps up on all of us so sadly one year he decided the North Sea crossing was too much hassle and put his boat up for sale. Carefully vetting would be purchasers he finally sold his pride and joy to a young couple who promised to look after her. Impressed by his tales of Holland they set forth and arrived in one of the old boy's favourite watering holes. Making sure the boat was safe and hiding the hatch key in the usual place they went shopping. On their return they were surprised to find the boat open with the cockpit full of elderly Dutchman drinking their beers. 'Who are you' they naturally enquired, 'who are you' the Dutch pensioners replied and 'where is old Bob'? After the young couple had explained the situation the old boys suitably embarrassed made to leave. 'Please stay' the couple said and thus inherited some new friends, not only in this port but the same in all of old Bobs haunts. It's a second hand yarn but in my books very believable and reinforces the kindness extended to our crowd over the years by our Dutch cousins.

Father his pockets swelled by his bank managers salary, was now manager of Hadleigh whose staff had got used to various Tickner sons sidling up to the counter with a hand up their jumpers supposedly looking like a gun demanding to see the manager. Anyway he bought a *Leisure 23* and named it Caravella on which he and mother continued their seafaring.

Father's middle name should have been 'bodger', he could never leave things alone he just had to add things on. Steps would appear on the coach roof, new electrical gadgets would be wired up using Bakelite switches, 'won't rust' he assured us. Bits of string led out of the engine box, pull this to start and this to stop read the instructions in pencil written on masking tape. Masking tape was his last bulk buy and used extensively particularly in the post for sealing letters and parcels. All of Dads modifications worked but would have made a yacht designer cringe.

Stone as I have said had little in the way of entertainment until a wine making club was formed whose membership quickly supplemented the European wine lake despite nightly wine tasting by all the members. The whole village bubbled and hubbled in sheds, greenhouses and conservatories. My poor Mum woke every morning with a hangover after breathing fermenting wine fumes all night!

One fine morning I rang Dad and suggested we might go for a sail on Caravella, 'capital idea' he boomed 'I'll bring along some of my wine and your mother can make sandwiches'. 'I'll bring a friend' said I and drove down to Stone. Father was waiting for us wearing one of his more unusual outfits. Wearing suits for work all week he liked to dress casually at weekends. Now casual for Pop means fancy dress to most people.

He has his pirates outfit, striped trousers and bandanna, his old man of the sea number, waders and yellow fisherman's souwester liberally covered in red antifouling, he looked like an abattoir worker. His desert rat ensemble was my favourite, beret, a vaguely military shirt and khaki flared shorts just like Eric Morecambe's! Pop would wear spots and stripes together with impunity, how we love him!

Seizing the dinghy's oars, two poles with paddle shaped planks nailed to them and ordering us to pull the dinghy we set off for the beach. Dad's dinghies have been a constant worry for us. Most sea accidents occur in dinghy's getting to and from the shore and Dad figured highly in those statistics. Not that Dad is a poor seaman far from it, it's more his choice of craft.

One year he famously bought a wooden and canvas collapsible tender designed to fold up and store in a small locker. Well it collapsed on a regular basis unfortunately whilst still some distance from the shore. Dad would swim around collecting the various components and stagger up the beach with them tucked neatly under his arm.

We noticed the sailing club car park was unusually full, 'it's a Snipe open meeting' Dad informed us. Snipes were a classic dinghy class, old men's boats the cadets would snigger, with one unusual feature a steel dagger board. At the risk of boring non-sailors I'll elaborate, dagger boards slotted into a casing and stopped sailboats going sideways. Modern dinghies had sliding boards mounted on a pivot allowing the board to lift if an obstruction was hit like the beach, sharks or a slow swimmer. The Snipes dagger board arrangement if snagged would probably lead to a capsize.

Striding through the club, father's outfit raised some eyebrows from the visiting yachtsmen but they got quickly back to tweaking their steeds. My friend a newcomer to all this was thoroughly enjoying his day, 'you know your Dads barking mad' he commented, 'you've not seen nothing yet' I replied 'the day is young'. Dad rowed strongly out to Caravella sitting bobbing on her mooring which was right on the start line ideal for watching the racing. 'Let's crack open some of my home made wine and watch these Snipe boys start' he suggested, an excellent idea we all agreed.

The ten minute gun went causing the yachts to start milling around, then the five which sent them into a frenzy of tacking and gybing all important pre start manoeuvres. Bang went the start gun and with a cacophony of shouting starboard, water and other such rules the fleet disappeared down the river.

Father, oblivious to all this had spotted something of much more interest. Backing dubiously down the slipway was a bright maroon Jag preceded by a huge powerboat with two monster Mercury outboards bolted to the transom. 'Obviously some East End boys made good' father muttered.

Now the beach shelves very slowly so you have to paddle some way before lowering the engines.

Two figures on the bow were paddling ineffectually to get into deep enough water to lower the outboards. Father rather fancies himself as the coxswain of a lifeboat, he was wearing the right uniform anyway. 'Hold on he roared, I'm coming to help', with that he leapt into the dinghy and rowed towards them at top speed.

'This should be good' I told my friend. 'Pass me a line' Dad ordered the hapless speedboaters, all they had was their ski rope, which they dutifully passed over. Dad rowed out to sea with the very long line paying out, eventually one hundred yards separated the two boats. The rope went taught and slowly very slowly they moved into deeper water. Unfortunately the tide had them in its grip and they began drifting towards the start line, which doubled up as the finish too. All this foolery had taken some time allowing the second phase of the catastrophe to develop.

Behind us the lead Snipes appeared around the headland, locked in a fierce battle to finish first, they were blissfully unaware of Dad's trip line strung right across the finish. Snagging the line one after another the Snipes rounded up, crews desperately trying to lift those metal boards, collided and capsized. Upside down boats littered the water with much shouting and bawling of wet frustrated crews. The last boat came into view saw the carnage and calmly sailed round the mess to get the winning gun.

Dad still rowing madly with his by now very confused tow drifted slowly out of sight. 'You were right' my pal agreed it did get much better. A while later as we enjoyed another home made beer there came the very loud sound of twin Mercury outboards. Over the horizon appeared the powerboat at breakneck speed towing Dad sitting calmly in the tiny dinghy spray flying everywhere clutching the ski tow rope. 'Thanks lads', he shouted as they stopped near to Caravella and calmly rowed back to us. Clambering aboard he commented 'I enjoyed that, lucky I was here to help them motor boat boys'. 'I expect you did Dad but I'm not sure about the Snipe boys' I replied.

With a puzzled shake of heads the motor boat crew waved and disappeared in a flurry of spray. Sitting in the Stone pub later that night we heard two men chatting to the barman. 'Hey John do you know a madman in fancy dress wot tows boats abaart'? We quickly finished our drinks and left through a side door.

Father doesn't own all the rights to eccentricity in

our family. Mother is a tad wacky herself and as for Mad Aunt Cicely she is in a class of her own. Cicely has always been about eighty, a mane of blonde hair topping a permanent tan from living in Ibiza complete with a crimson slash of lipstick. She is Mums second cousin and completely insane. She appeared in music halls around Britain with Max Wall, the Crazy Gang and others of that era. She was as strong as an Ox and could drink anyone under the table. On a holiday in Ibiza one year she took us to an ex pat party which was exceedingly liquid and afterwards delivered me and my pals home one at a time draped across the back of her moped before going into town for a proper drink!

Everyone was 'Daaarrling' including her second husband Manuel. Cicely told her suitor she was seventy, he said sixty, they both lied. Add ten years to both and you were nearer the truth. They moved to the Spanish mainland to Manuel's ranch where he kept a string of ex polo horses. For an income she ran Wild West days with her husband and his sons staging mock gunfights and falling off the horses. Cicely was the barmaid dispensing liquor in their cowboy saloon, all this at the age of eighty!

Mother has aspirations of being a painter, her watercolours of flowers are terrific but anything with legs are a no go. To get around this artistic deficiency she paints objects in front of her subjects. Hence you get titles such as sheep behind hay bale or cow behind hedgerow. Her current favourite are pigs, so pigs lying down or pigs in a trough, you get the idea. Every year her painting class holds an art exhibition in Burnham village hall and every year she is delighted to sell at least two works of art always to an anonymous buyer.

My parents loft by the way is stacked with hundreds of her pictures hidden in a dark corner, good old Dad.

Joff, the middle brother followed Dad into the bank

but quickly tired of it, especially as Jeremy and I were having such a good time at sea. He left, took a two week catering course and within months was a junior purser on the Windsor Castle. Buster the youngest was not so lucky, he spent several years stuck behind a bank counter before escaping to become a gentleman of the road, not a tramp but a commercial traveller as reps were known in those days.

Talking of tramps reminds me of an encounter with a particularly ragged one. When the folks moved to Stone they decided to drag the old cardboard caravan, scene of many a crime out from the site it had lodged in for twenty five years. Protesting strongly it followed Dad's car up the road where we eventually hid it behind some trees at the bottom of the parent's garden.

For years it became the overflow dormitory for young cadets at open meetings. Mom and Dad would keep an eye on them, give them breakfast and let them use the bathroom in the house. Yet another generation of kids having fun in our old van all through my parent's kindness. Much later Dad's homemade wine stock was moved into the van which allowed Dads pals to wine taste and fall over in peace.

One Halloween two teenage girls who had often enjoyed the vans hospitality asked Mum and Dad if they could use the van as they were going to a Halloween party at the sailing club, 'of course' they chorused, 'Guy will light the gas lamp for you and pull out the beds'.

Buster arriving home later was told about the girls and decided to try a little haunting. Pulling a sheet over his head he crept down the garden, saw the flickering gas lamp was still on, wrenched the door open and shouted 'wooooooooo' whilst waving his arms about. Fortunately the girls had found alternative not so spartan accommodation elsewhere but a passing tramp attracted by the light thought he had found heaven and was half way through his second bottle of Dads wine. Jumping up the bearded raggedly dressed tramp shouting help bolted out of the door jumped a ditch and disappeared across the field. Not that Buster saw any of this he had fled back up the garden in a blue funk back to the arms of his mummy!

My experience with a tramp was whilst hitching to see my beloved. Underneath Upminster bridge lived an old tramp that I got to know, as it was a convenient place to hitch out of the rain. He was an ex company director who had got tired of the rat race and one day just walked away and started to paint. He had an old fashioned pram in which he placed his paintings and pushed it to Romford every day to sell in the market. Who's to say he was wrong?

Back at college, life in my new digs on the farm was idyllic in comparison to my previous lodgings. Great food, my own bedroom, I could watch the TV whenever I wanted and with my little Triumph Herald sitting in the drive I was at last mobile. The farmer kept as a hobby Arabian stallions, well big black horses, I'm not particularly up in equine matters. He used to disappear at great speed down the road sitting on a gig towed by one of the monsters with shiny brass bits and a polished leather halter. Hanging on next to him was his young son.

A by product of horses is manure which he loaded into an old cart pulled by a more sedate steed and sold door to door around the local neighbourhood. The father drove and parked the horse outside client's houses sending the little boy to clinch the deal. The young lad's sales pitch was succinct and to the point if not a trifle too direct, 'want to buy some horse shit madam' he would enquire with his angelic face tilted becomingly. Not many housewives could refuse his charms!

College work had become harder, more time on theory less time in the workshop pulling engines about and exams at the end of every term. Time flew by and there I was sitting the finals. An eight-hour technical drawing exam was the last test. Eight hours, you could build a ship in less time. The examination board quickly informed each student how they had done so the shipping companies could organise their newly qualified crews.

So there I stood, a completed apprenticeship under my belt, a bit of paper stating I had passed my part A second engineering ticket and four years of my life gone. It was a strange feeling saying goodbye to my fellow students who rapidly dispersed throughout the four corners of the world. Little did I know I was never to meet any of them again as we promised to keep in touch and waved goodbye.

Passenger Ship Day's

The Windsor Castle

I drove my little car for the last time out of Southampton to see my girlfriend. She was happy to see me finish college as every Monday morning for the last two years she had woken me up, made me tea and sent me on my way back to work at the ungodly hour of five in the morning.

My company, keen to realise the investment in time and money made in my training quickly sent me my new ships joining instructions. I was to report in one month's time in Southampton as junior engineer on the Windsor Castle! There is a God, the best choice possible.

My cargo ship uniform besides having shrunk, well it didn't fit anymore, was too scruffy for passenger ships. With Mum in tow we went up to Leadenhall Street in the city of London which was the heart of the British shipping industry. All the shipping companies head offices were based here and several naval outfitters, as they were so grandly known.

'I'd like a complete outfit for my son' ordered Mother, I think she thought I was going back to school.

A little man with a tape measure around his neck and dandruff scurried here and there into dusty corners pulling out various bits of uniform. A navy blue reefer jacket and trousers for Sundays in colder climates. A navy bum freezer jacket with a pointy bit at the back joined at the front by two gold buttons on a short chain for weekdays in the cold and a matching white one for hot climates and my favourite white Number Tens for Sunday in the tropics. This consisted of a long sleeved jacket with epaulets and white long trousers bottomed off with white socks and shoes.

I liked this outfit when I tried it on in front of my mirror back home. I looked like Richard Gere in An Officer and a Gentleman, some hope!

Short sleeved white shirt with epaulettes shorts with long socks completed the tropical daytime look. Various other sundry items were added to the pile, dress white shirts, cummerbund, uniform black brogues, nearly as bad as *Start Rites* and a proper tie it yourself bow tie.

Me ,Jimmy our steward and a good looking officer SA Vaal

It came to a month salary but I think good old Mum picked up the bill. My old boiler suits were in rags and my engine room boots looked like something a clown wore. A quick visit to the Army and Navy store soon rectified the situation. Loaded down with my new purchases and some 'civvy' clothes I boarded a train to Southampton.

Nothing could prepare me for the sight that greeted me at the dockside. Pandemonium reigned. Bits of engine swinging about on cranes, frozen carcasses on pallets fork lifted into holds, chippers chipping rust from the hull suspended on precarious gantries and painters with brushes on long poles painting the famous lavender hull. This was the day before the passengers arrived, how in heavens name was the ship going to leave on time.

I had been used to my tiny Clan Ross, which had no set sailing schedule, left when it could and arrived later. Due to fluctuating fruit prices we would often slow down to dock a few days later to take advantage of a price hike in bananas!

On Union Castle ships you had to leave and arrive at each designated port not only on a set day but also at an exact time. You could set your calendar and watch by our arrivals and departures. We would leave Southampton on a Friday cross the Bay of Biscay bound for Las Palmas to bunker cheap fuel oil. Some eleven days later we would arrive in Cape Town for an overnight stop to refuel, discharge and load cargo. Passengers would leave us in Cape Town to be replaced by South Africans who would sail up coast with us.

Port Elizabeth and East London were our two other stops before the bright lights of Durban for three days. The return trip down coast took in all the same ports before the two week passage back to Southampton, the whole voyage lasting six weeks.

Union Castle had five passenger mail ships on this run. The Windsor Castle was the newest and biggest and also the flagship of the fleet. The SA Vaal previously named the Transvaal Castle but due to our links with SAF marine had been renamed and painted in SAF marines livery. The Pendennis Castle, affectionately known as the penis castle, the Edinburgh and the old girl of the fleet the Oranje, the orange box.

Wagonloads of Royal Mail under strict security were secreted away into locked holds along with some impressive amounts of gold bullion. Naive little me thought there were sanctions in place against South Africa.

Hauling my gear up the crew gangway I found myself in a maze of alleyways, the carpets covered with lining to protect them from the onslaught of shore side workers who had the ship in pieces. Panels and whole walls were lying everywhere with men in boiler suits with Vosper's emblazoned on them hammering and welding with great gusto.

This was the accommodation, what would the engine room be like? I was soon to find out. I found an officer's notice board with instructions for my accommodation. Junior Engineer Tickner, day work, cabin 52 port side. Not understanding the significance of this notice I blithely made my way upward to the officer's quarters to be greeted by two dwarves. Well Arthur and Jimmy as they introduced themselves weren't really dwarves but they were vertically restricted as we now have to say in this PC world. These guys were the officer's stewards. Arthur old, bald and resembling Arthur Askey complete with accent and laugh and Jimmy young and impressionable.

They turned out to be real diamonds and soon were digging me out of all sorts of scrapes. Dumping my gear on my cabin floor I took stock of my surroundings. I had a sailor size bed, not double but enough for two! A day couch which ran at right angles to the other so providing an alternative kipping arrangement to allow for the ships pitching or rolling.

I had a wardrobe to hang my uniform, draws under the bed and a desk with chair. A sink was provided for ablutions and emergency loo should the communal heads prove too much of an effort. Don't look at me like that, stand up the man who hasn't at least once availed himself with a sink.

There were power points scattered around the room, but the walls were bare except for bits of blue tack and cellotape, previously fixing posters I supposed. Three empty bottles of scotch clinked under the bed as the ship gently moved against her mooring lines, a testimony to my predecessor's alcohol consumption.

Arthur knocked on my door, 'first engineer wants to see you in his cabin now' he said. Following his instructions I wound my way up to the top deck and walked along the passageway reading the signs on the doors. Captain's Day Cabin, Commodores private suite, First Engineers day Cabin. I had only been on the boat five minutes and I was already in the inner sanctum.

The first's door burst open, 'you must be Robin come in' said a short dark haired man beaming. I didn't know this man from Adam, what was going on. 'Have a drink, Joff tells me you sup rum, I think I'll join you', waving me to a chair he busied himself making the drinks. Suddenly all was clear, the big brother syndrome this time in the shape of Joff had again worked its magic, I had forgotten that Joff was a fellow officer on the Windsor.

'Joff and I get on really well he said, 'surprising really, as he's a Purser' and introduced himself, 'Dave Hill pleased to meet you. I will be in charge of you so it's important we get on well'.

'You and another Junior are on day work' he continued 'which is as it sounds, work during the day and have every night off, it's the best number on the ship so don't fuck up'! He also warned me that several of the more experienced engineers would be jealous of our privileged jobs and would make it tough for us. He added some more advice that I would get some flack having a purser as a brother, thus I was introduced to shipboard politics.

'Go and find your way around the engine room and make yourself useful'. So ended my first of many meetings with this talented and generous senior officer.

Stopping off in my cabin I pulled on my pristine boiler suit and feeling like a new boy at school opened the door marked Engine room. Expecting to be hit by a wall of noise and steam the ensuing silence was eerie. A gentle hum from far down below was all I could hear. There was a mesh gate marked lift in front of me with metal stairs on one side leading down into the gloom. I thought I would take the stairs and start my education of the ships structure.

It was a bloody long way down, on my way I passed exits marked Cinema, First Class deck, gym, tourist class and kitchens amongst others. These exits subsequently became my secret way of moving around the ship avoiding the Master at Arms and senior officers who would not be impressed with my choice of companions.

Eventually I arrived on the main engine room platform, literally my breath was taken away with the feverish activity before me. A control board spanning nearly the width of the ship was full of red and green lights, alarm sirens were wailing and steam was hissing from a multitude of valves. Great round dials with arrows quivering with steam pressure shone in the glare of the workmen's floodlights the whole engine space was full of shore side workers.

On the Clan Ross all maintenance and repair work was carried out by the officers. The Castle ships because of their tight schedules relied on Vosper's and other specialist engineering companies to board the ship as soon as it docked, rip it apart and stick it back together in ten days. It was always a close run thing!

The Clan Ross had been a diesel ship, this monster was driven by two huge steam turbines fuelled by three boilers that stretched from the ships plates to the top of the funnel. I knew nothing about steam except you could iron with it, this was certainly going to be a steep learning curve.

Sticking out from the control panel were two pairs of gleaming stainless steel wheels two on the port side and two to starboard. Just above them were the ships telegraphs, so this was how you manoeuvred I surmised. The great green steam turbines towered above the main platform, littered with steam valves it was awe inspiring, how I was ever going to understand what everything or anyone did.

I clattered down some steps to plate level to find bilge and oil pumps in pieces surrounded by earnest looking men checking their watches, time was getting tight. Oily water swilled about the bilge's, it was a fineable offence to pump bilge's over the side polluting the harbour water so working conditions were wet as well as noisy and hot.

I walked aft through several open water tight doors, memories of Second World War submarine films with trapped seamen crossed my mind. I emerged into another large engine space full of compressors and multi-coloured pipes disappearing through deck heads and bulkheads. This was the freezer flat which cooled all the refrigerated holds full of best British beef and

New Zealand lamb

Continuing aft following the propeller shaft I past the huge stabiliser rams which were being coated with waterproof grease from five gallon barrels. Finally I reached the stern tubes where the two mighty shafts passed through lignae vitae glands into the sea to drive the propellers. Seawater poured from the glands, designed to cool and lubricate the shafts and would be adjusted with giant spanners once we were at sea. At least there were some pieces of machinery I recognised, all be it they were several times the size I was used to.

I retraced my steps going forward into the boiler room dodging the workers lifting, welding and hammering with feverish intent. This was the powerhouse of the whole ship and where most repair work needed to be done.

Super heated steam needs great technical skills to harness and utilise safely. Massive amounts of specialist packing and lagging were employed to ensure safety and efficiency. Sadly, sometimes human errors led to tragedy in boiler rooms.

The most forward part of the engine room was the generator flat. The Clan Ross had tiny Rolls Royce turbo generators about the size of a family saloon. The Windsor had three diesel generators the size of London buses and three steam turbines of similar size, which were used when at sea. A working platform at the same height as the top of the 'gennys' hosted a similar sized control panel to the main engine room.

Massive circuit breakers with two handed wooden handles for insulation would put the 'gennys' on line looking for the entire world like something to shock Frankenstein into life. Great dials indicating voltage and amperage for each machine surrounded these breakers, it was a king sized version of your fuse box under the stairs at home.

A second engineer spotted my wanderings and came over to me, after we had introduced ourselves he allocated me some steam valves to repack and sent me off to the stores to get tools and packing. A brown-coated store man, well I never, issued me with what I needed and I set to.

The procedure for the task was first make sure the valve is isolated then burn yourself, well that's what I did anyway! Remove top nut and hand wheel, undo two nuts holding down gland follower, the studs usually came out as well, dig out old burnt packing with sharpened welding rod. Burn yourself again, and as I haven't sworn for the last three pages, fucking hell that bastards hot, now I feel better for that.

Cut packing at correct angle and length so it fits snugly, press around valve spindle and tighten down with gland follower. Not so bad a job you would think, wrong. Undo nuts again, remove gland follower, cut packing and place at thirty degrees to first ring and repeat until gland is fully packed and reassemble. If it reads boring you should try it yourself.

All around me engineers were repacking valves in minutes, they must have asbestos hands I thought. It was not a job to bodge however, if you did then the bloody thing would leak and piss steam until the next time the boilers were shut down. Many a valve haunted me for weeks as I passed by ducking the escaping steam. Actually I became quite competent after a couple of false starts, maybe all that time in college wasn't wasted after all.

Another short man wearing a beret appeared it was the Chief Engineer on his final inspection. He appeared satisfied with the shore side work and knocked us off leaving the engineers on watch to fire up the boilers and raise steam for our departure in the morning.

Going up in the lift I felt for the first time that I had

something tangible to offer, at last a real job, not as a cadet but as a bona fide engineer.

Arthur gave me a message from my brother to join him for drinks at eight in his cabin then up the road for a meal. After a shower I donned civvies and found my way down to the purser's cabins. Opening the door into their alleyway I was struck by a wall of music issuing from open cabin doors, the loudest coming from Joffs.

Standing at his doorway I looked in to see a mass of people swigging and talking furiously. Joff spotted me standing there and dragging me in pressed a fortunately cold beer into my sore hands and introduced me to the mob. They were all pursers and purserettes, what did they all do? Clan boats only had one, what a lot I have to learn I thought.

After a short burst of speed drinking we lurched up the road for more of the same and food. No brothels for these sophisticated officers but off to the Juniper Berry a gay pub which happened to serve good food.

The next morning nursing a slightly creaky head, I was put on the shake by Neil the other junior engineer ready for our first morning of day work. Neil Lang, which was soon changed to Clang due to his propensity for dropping clangers had a dark secret, just like the character played by Benny Hill in the Italian Job he had a passion for big woman, and not a lot of people know that.

We met the first engineer Dave in the officer's mess and over tea and toast served by Arthur and Jimmy he outlined our jobs.

At six each morning we were to walk the deck noting any problems with the machinery, winches derricks and the like. Starting in the Chinese laundry right at the aft end of the ship we had to inspect the various machines, washers and dryers and fill out a report.

The crew, tourist and first class kitchens were next to survey and finally a visit to the purser's bureau to make sure their 'Gestetner' copiers were working. This was my favourite stop as the purserettes were stunning. We also had to receive reports from the passenger stewards about any mechanical or plumbing problems in their passenger's cabins. Once we had a full list we would report back to Dave and he would allocate our jobs.

Today as it was our first trip we were to go below for standby and watch the engineer's fire up the boilers and get the turbines up to speed. Keeping well out of the way I watched as sirens blared, ships telegraphs rang and engineers spun the steel wheels. The turbines began to hum as they were fed steam from the boilers and slowly we were on our way. Dave Hill sidled over to me and said 'get up top quick and watch us pulling away from the dock, it's quite a sight'.

Running to the lift and out on to the deck I watched as the gap widened between ship and shore with two tugs fussing round us. The decks and dock were lined with people. Some of the passengers had thrown paper streamers to their loved ones on the dock which tightened then broke and fluttered gently down to the sea. Leaving port means so many things to different people. The folk left behind clutching the remains of the streamers would be sad, the people on board also sad but elated because it was the start of a new beginning in a new land. For some it was the beginning of a two or six week holiday and for others it was the only way to get to South Africa for business as few airlines flew there. For me it was the start of a new adventure, something I had trained for all those years.

Some thirty years later on my sailboat Wizzo I still get the same sense of adventure when leaving port and landfall is always special. At this moment the 11th of

May 2002 I am one hundred and fifty miles from Horta in the Azores after sailing from Antigua sixteen days and two thousand miles ago.

My crew all first timers are buzzing with expectation and the fulfilment of a dream, crossing the Atlantic under sail. I just feel that time has stood still and I am once again standing on that deck watching Southampton slipping away.

True to the first engineers prediction some hairy arsed prat of a time served engineer cornered me and told me I wouldn't know what engineering was like until I had spent ten years on watch and added that all pursers were poofs! As he was built like the proverbial brick shithouse I didn't take issue. I hope he was suitably put down by my contemptuous sniff admittedly made when his back was turned!

First night at sea, what bloody uniform to wear, Arthur to the rescue, blues mate that's what the rig of the day is blues. Pulling on the new reefer jacket, trousers and those awful shoes I realised they needed running in. As I squeaked down the alleyway I portrayed a square cut manly image, the blue serge uniform was like cardboard with no give in it abrading my body where it touched and it looked oh so new.

Dinner for officers was served in the First class dining saloon, a huge room with wide windows looking out over the sea and beautifully decorated. A sweeping staircase deposited you next to the junior officer's table without having to thread your way through the mass of elegantly clad passengers.

Each senior officer had his own table where already I could see fine South African wine and good conversation flowing. I joined our table and was soon introduced to mates, pursers, electricians and radio officers who were either off watch or day workers like me.

The menu was extensive reminding me of my last fine meal in Brentwood so I stayed clear of the fish!

One of the mates advised me to keep off decks for a couple of days to let the talent sort itself out. Further explanations were needed. All the young girls travelled in tourist class sharing four to a cabin, sometimes there was a rich bird in first class but that was rare. Apparently all the single male passengers would chase the single girls for the first two nights. If successful, unless they had very understanding cabin mates or a girl who liked it al fresco behind the lifeboats, then consummation was impossible. 'That's where we come in' said the third mate with a grin.

'Case the talent at the Captains cocktail party then introduce yourself in the tourist bar later, buy them a drink and invite them to the disco, never fails'.

Being new to this game I thanked him for his advice and bought him a drink whilst pumping for more insider information.

Tired out after a long day's valve packing I excused myself and went back to my cabin. I couldn't help noticing the other officer's uniforms as I passed by. No one was wearing anything like mine. Flared bottoms with high Chelsea boots, tailored twin pleated jackets, button down shirts with kipper ties all tied with an enormous knot. They all looked like Jason King whilst I looked like Norma Wisdom, first chance ashore I was up for a change of image.

The Chinese laundry first thing in the morning was interesting. All the machines were steam driven and all leaked, maintenance was going to be interesting I thought.

'Washing machine very fucked' said one inscrutable vest and short clad laundry man, I fix I said and hit it with a hammer, 'velly good you young plick' was all the thanks I got.

The kitchens were also steam driven so valves, glands and pipes were our main problem, repairs being undertaken usually in the middle of the breakfast rush. Stewards dodging round us with heaped plates of breakfast with chefs doing what chefs do so well shouting at the top of their voices.

It was all so different to anything I had ever experienced before. College had taught me how to change a fuel injector not how to mend a washing machine or huge industrial oven.

I enjoyed walking out on deck for some sun and fresh air each morning to blow away the cobwebs. Examining the winches and hatches could usually be spun out for at least an hour before 'smoko' up in the officer's mess. Time then for a fag and catch up with the ships gossip with Arthur and Jimmy.

We had to wear clean white boiler suits when on deck or in the accommodation so as not to offend the passengers. Once a tan was acquired it's surprising how the top few buttons come undone exposing ones hairy chest, enough to quicken the heart beat of a fair maiden I reasoned.

Next stop the purser's bureau for some banter with the girls and a chat with my brother. It was surprising how often their Gestetner copiers broke down, these were the days before photocopiers. The machines had big handles like wringers, one turn one copy all very time consuming.

At midday I had a quick shower and more fine food at the officers table and still time for an hour's sunbathe then back to work, no wonder the watch keepers were jealous!

Heeding my new friend's advice I stayed off deck until the Captains cocktail party which was held in the ballroom. I went for a trial run to the first class party standing politely in full dress uniform accepting every drink that was offered and chatting politely to ageing dowagers and old colonial types.

I thought I caught a glimpse of something young but there was such a throng of offices round her I didn't get to see her face. Later that evening I attended the tourist class bash, this was more like it, young things in tight things giggling and supping faster than I was.

So unfortunately were the more experienced officers, straight in for the kill leaving me circling around the periphery like a short-sighted shark with no prey.

After dinner I wandered around the first class bars and library enjoying the old fashioned feel of prosperity, wooden panels and bright lights setting off the fine clothes and jewels of the obviously well heeled passengers. A huddle of officers were in a corner of the library talking animatedly to someone in their midst. I wandered over and watched the back of a very pretty girl dealing effortlessly with the advances made by the officers and gentlemen.

The crowd thinned as one by one they were refused until finally she turned sensing me behind her. She was stunning, 'hello' she said 'you must be new', did the uniform stand out that much I wondered but before I could answer the remaining guys closed ranks for a final assault on the poor girl.

Not wanting to look a complete fool I made my way to the bar and ordered a drink, 'may I have a gin and tonic' said a small voice behind me, the vision had finally defeated the last hopeful and wanted to have a drink with me!

I admitted it was my first trip and we talked about everything and nothing as Mills and Boon would have it. Later she asked me to escort her to the dance where the ships bands were belting out some modern dance tunes. We danced and she held on tight, was this a dream I thought but I had failed to see the envious looks from the spurned officers or the raised eyebrows of the senior staff.

When we parted she kissed me lightly on the cheek and said 'can I see you tomorrow and maybe perhaps we could see in the dawn'? I floated on air back to my empty cabin little knowing thunderclouds were in the air.

I had a terse interview with my boss the next morning along the lines of 'well done for pulling that first class cracker but here are the rules. Don't dance closely, don't snog on the dance floor, don't hold hands, don't be seen in passenger accommodation' and so on, there was a very long list of don'ts. I had been put well and truly straight.

Fearing there was an even longer list of don'ts I went to see Joff, the jungle drums had forewarned him of my success and bollocking so we celebrated and commiserated over a beer whilst he gave me more rules.

Never be seen leaving a passenger cabin and keep on the good side of the master at arms were top of his lists. Master at Arms were the nautical equivalents of night watchman with additional security responsibilities I suppose they were the ships police. They had set rounds marked with boxes in which they inserted a key, which logged the time of inspection.

One of the boxes was in the officer's accommodation so heeding my brother's advice early that evening I left my cabin door open and waylaid John the duty master at arms. Beckoning him in and offering a beer I introduced myself. 'I know your brother well' he said taking an appreciative gulp of his beer, 'got him out of many a hole'. It was the first of many beers we shared and in due course they paid off.

After dinner I went to meet my blonde, 'let's talk on

deck' I said and gave her the rundown on the ships rules. 'How stupid' she said with a voice that sent shivers down my spine. Her father was German and her mother French, fortunately she erred on her mother's side with a delightful French accent.

'Perhaps after the disco we could go to your cabin so no one can see us'. I found it difficult to walk after that comment, erections can so hamper forward movement. Suddenly I remembered the bareness of my cabin, no soft lights, no music and no drink, could I borrow some of Joffs, probably busy himself I reasoned. Suddenly I had a brain wave.

The previous afternoon Neil from the next cabin had invited me in to show pictures of his wife and whilst trapped he produced a tape machine and plugged me into an ear socket. I had to listen to his loving wife wishing him good night but I had also seen on his desk a stack of music tapes.

With an idea fermenting in my head I danced at the regulatory distance from the vision until she said take me to your cabin. Walking nonchalantly over the deck, she was first class so she was street legal all the way to our entry door, checking the coast was clear we ducked into my cabin. 'Make yourself comfortable' I suggested, I had previously wrapped a red handkerchief around my bedside light to give some kind of ambience, 'I'll be back in a minute'.

Silently opening Neil's cabin door I saw him sound asleep with his little tape machine faithfully sitting next to him. Pocketing a couple of tapes I gently lifted the machine and started to back out. Suddenly there was resistance and Neil stirred, the bastard still had the lead plugged in his ear.

Lust was upon me so with a tug and a loud pop I had my music and he an empty ear. Modesty prevents me from too much detail but we listened to Neil's music until the batteries ran down. Just before dawn as the pink fingers of light came creeping across the calm sea she said, 'would you mind taking off my black dress', of course I wasn't wearing it, I didn't start that sort of thing for years, as she turned her back inviting me to unzip her. The little scrap of black material had a Dior label on it and that's the last I thing I remember until she slipped away with a promise of see you by the pool later.

I had one final task that long night, get that earpiece back into Neil's head, mission accomplished I slept the sleep of a happy young man.

We had many nights like the first, my cup runneth over, the only thing marring my joy was Neil's constant grumbling about these modern batteries only lasting five minutes.

One evening I received an invitation to meet the visions Father in a small private function room. He welcomed me in, poured me a drink and bade me sit down. He said he was glad that his daughter and I were having such a good time, that she always told him everything and that she had had a bad experience with a man recently which he had sorted out.

I wasn't sure where this conversation was going but I understood quite clearly how he could sort things out. He ran a huge company and power hung easily on his broad shoulders.

'She tells me you are sleeping with her'. How do you answer that, it was definitely on the list of officer's don'ts,' but if you make her happy then her mother and I are also happy'. Seems we are all one happy family I thought but said 'you have a beautiful daughter and I promise to look after her'.

He rang a bell and in walked his wife and the vision, breathing a sigh of relief I smiled at the girl as she held my hand, well lets all enjoy the rest of the trip said the father interview over.

Now some of you might think I am a callous bastard without feelings but I tell you she touched my heart and nearly changed my life. Just before we reached Cape Town I had another interview with her father, 'do you want to come and work for my new company' he asked. Well she was beautiful and South Africa was a great country but I was young and to be honest had too many wild oats still to sow

I waved them sadly good bye as they climbed into a Rolls Royce on the dockside and watched the vision drive out of the dock and out of my life.

I apologise for the length and depth of this relationships narrative but out of all the many people I met on the passenger ships she was the only one who nearly made me swallow the anchor and yes I did buy Neil a box of new batteries.

So up the coast we went, first stop Port Elizabeth just a night's sail away. Now the rules were different on the coast my ever-friendly third mate informed me. No Captains cockers to vet the new passengers who had boarded in Cape Town, just straight down to the tourist class bar and away you go.

In those long ago days South Africa not only had Apartheid they also had very tight restrictions on what you could see at the cinema, listen to on the radio and enjoy at the theatre. Can you believe they censored the Goon show and cut half an hour off 'No sex please were' British'. There was no gambling and no drinking on a Sunday unless you were dining. Altogether a totally repressed country!

Scattered throughout the ship were one-armed bandits, the South Africans would form a queue down the alleyways and wait patiently for their go. And can you believe this, the most popular entertainment put on by the officers was bingo, classified by their government as gambling but on a British ship legal.

Joff and I used to run the bingo, he would work the ping-pong ball machine and we would take it in turns to call the numbers but very, very badly. For instance, two fat ladies, one, two and six, five, six and nine, sixty-nine kindly leave the room sir. All of these calls went clean over the head of Mr and Mrs Van De Merwe.

The ship's entertainment left much to be desired. It was a cross between 'Hi de Hi' and 'It ain't half hot Mum'. There were two resident ballroom dancers who gave lessons and dancing shows aided by the ships band or orchestra, as they liked to be known. None of the band was in there first flush of youth but they bashed the old music out with great gusto every night. On gala nights they would set up at the bottom of the sweeping staircase into the first class dining saloon.

All the senior officers would get invites to pre dinner cocktail parties, some handled them better than others. On one infamous occasion the chief radio officer who was not adverse to the odd gin and tonic stood at the top of the dining room steps preparing himself for his entrance.

As he took his first unsteady step on the staircase the ship rolled and he fell all the way down taking out the band on his way through. The drums and cymbals clashed and clattered across the floor, the double bass trapped its owner and the trumpeter caught the guitarist somewhere he shouldn't of. The slightly bemused officer stood up brushed himself down and continued his way to his table seemingly oblivious to the chaos all around him. We on the junior officer's table were up for a round of applause but decorum won the day.

The dining room on reflection provided us minions with many happy hours of entertainment, some quite macabre.

Many elderly and infirm people travelled on the

Castle boats, some to escape the British winter on a six-week round trip whilst others left us in Cape Town to join the Blue train. This steam locomotive took the inland route across the Karoo, a desert area, and on up to Johannesburg. They would often rejoin the ship for the trip home having experienced some of the beautiful South African hinterland.

Many of the infirm were wheelchair bound looked after by a companion or nurse who would escort them to the dining room. Old Robby the lift attendant would by prior well tipped appointment meet them on their floor and whisk them down for their meals. Abandoning his lift he would guide their chairs through to their table, apply the wheel brake and attach the securing chain to an eyebolt under the table to the chair.

Deftly pocketing his tip Robby went off to collect his next poor soul.

I wondered for a long time who earns most money on the ships. I found out when I saw how certain members of the crew were met back in Southampton. The maitre de was collected by a chauffeur in a 'Rolls', old Robby's wife picked him up in a Porsche and the Captain caught a train home. To watch the maitre de was pure magic in fact Paul Daniels couldn't make a tip disappear quicker!

He organised the passenger tables, who and where they wanted to dine which officer to sit with and which waiter to serve them. Special menus were available and the best wine could flow, all it took was a little greasing of the palm as you dined on your first night and when he bade you bon voyage on your way out after your last supper.

There may have been freemasons meetings at sea but I know that the Buffaloes met often, a fact told me with great glee by my donkey man who was apparently head buffalo or equivalent. His source of joy was because the Captain was very much his junior in this organisation, 'rank doesn't pull all the strings' he would exclaim smiling smugly.

Let's get back to the wheelchairs. The occupants sat securely lashed to the floor, brake applied, let the ship roll I'll be all right thought the passenger. Unfortunately some of the incumbents were a trifle overweight placing unfair strains on the security measures. A tremendous roll of the ship could with luck make the chair and table part company and off the chair would go with a howling occupant on board still clutching his knife and fork.

If you have ever played pinball in an amusement arcade you would have an idea of the chairs passage around the room. Cannoning off other diners gaining speed on the downward roll it would take several determined waiters to eventually corner and stop the runaway chair.

A slightly more sinister form of entertainment was when a passenger failed to finish his meal and I don't mean he was too full. Due to the large number of very old passengers a certain percentage never made it past their starters. There were many occasions when diners ended up head down in the soup.

Now obviously this put a bit of a dampener on the occasion but it also created a work up for the engineers, let me explain. In those days burials at sea were the norm otherwise we would arrive in port with freezers crammed with stiffs, not a pleasant thought.

To enable the deceased to be committed to the deep with decorum the ship at six in the morning would slow right down for the coffin to be slipped gently from under their national flag. The sorrowful widow would sadly wave her loved one goodbye before a restorative nip of brandy with friends in the Captains quarters.

We down below in the engine room would have

spent two hours slowing the turbines down a complicated procedure which wasn't like just taking your foot of a car accelerator. Once the body had departed, the bridge would ring for half ahead then full steam ahead leaving just a ripple and a memory behind.

On one occasion the second engineer was a trifle energetic with the full steam ahead pushing the stops fully open. The ship surged forward with a massive bow and stern wave. The bereaved still with her hand in mid air gasped with astonishment as her husband reappeared, his coffin surfing on the ships wake, 'funny' she said 'Arthur could never hang ten when he was alive'!

There was one memorable occasion at the final night party, which coincided with a wedding reception, the wedding ceremony having been conducted by the Captain. Speeches made the guests were in mid chorus of Auld Lang Syne. Old granddad Bert full of fine brandy was entering into the spirit of things when his spirit left him.

No one noticed his demise and for a full ten minutes he was dragged in and out until they broke company for the knees bend arms raised 'RA RA RA'. At this stage he fell to the floor. The bride being a nurse spent her wedding night not in the arms of her new husband but giving the poor old boy the kiss of life which sadly failed!

Besides the dancers and band there was a ships photographer who would snap passengers at the fancy dress evenings and any other occasion where he could flog a photo with the ships logo on it. Hairdressers ran a natty line in blue rinses, shopkeepers flogged little plastic models of Castle liners and a physio tried to keep passengers fit in his tiny gym or running them around the deck. He was later sacked as they found his horse stuffed with Ganga. I don't mean a real horse I mean the type of horse that Dicky Attenborough and fellow Stalag prisoners used to jump over whilst digging for freedom.

There was a small cinema and a disco DJ'd by pursers and occasionally me, High Ho silver lining could usually get the 'yarpies' jumping around like lunatics.

The real entertainment was organised by the pursers which is where 'it ain't half hot Mum' comes in. We held gala dinners on deck by the illuminated swimming pool. The band strummed away under the tropical starry sky with always the chance of an inebriated passenger falling in or a runaway wheelchair fancying a swift midnight dip.

Fancy dress evenings went down well especially themed ones like vicars and tarts. Scantily dressed tarts and vicars with their arses hanging out were commonplace. My favourite theme, what were you wearing when the ship went down, usually produced at least one passenger with his pants around his ankles clutching a loo seat and toilet paper!

Bingo and whist drives were always well attended especially by the yarpies but the real attractions were the shows performed by the pursers and a handful of other aspiring thespians, myself included.

I suppose the most famous act we put on was the Ada Grunsworthy School of Dancing Extravaganza, as the notices pinned up all round the ship would have it. The passengers would buzz with excitement for days, a professional dance troupe performing intricate new dance moves for them to enjoy and perhaps emulate later whilst cutting the rug.

Little did they know we spent hours up in the officer's games room practising the Pasadoble, Waltz and the Galloping Major under the tutorage of the professional dancers. One difference to most dance troupes, ours was guys only with tall officers as girls dancing with short ones as male partners.

To add spice and realism to the occasion we the girls, well I never, would wear bright yellow ballroom gowns, big blonde wigs engine room boots with bows on and about four inches of makeup. The men wore outfits loosely based on some remote Ruritanian navy uniform with chest full of spurious yet impressive medals.

The ballroom was hushed as the troupe was announced, lights were dimmed, elderly ladies quietly fanning themselves in anticipation.

With a fanfare and a splash of lights we charged onto the floor roses in mouths heads held high pasadobling for all we were worth. It didn't stop there we glided and swooped in perfect formation through our well choreographed routine ending with a final flourish to the roars of our quite frankly bemused audience.

The Ada Grunsworthy dance troupe SA Vaal

We actually bashed and banged our way around the floor often cannoning off each other but for me it was show business, you know what they say the roar of the grease paint and the smell of the crowd.

Standing in a line with drooping moustaches, trays and long aprons we would regale the passengers with drinking songs as the singing waiters. Wearing ribbons bells and straw hats we would knock seven bells out of each other with sticks, in the strange way that Morris dancers do.

The troupe in action

Sometimes full of beer we would put together a 'skiffle' group with penny whistles, wash boards and a packing case with a stick and strings attached. We would try to sing mournful Irish ditties and slightly risqué country songs. Kenneth Williams's character 'Rambling Sid Rumpole' was our mentor! Another act was a song called 'if I was not upon the sea' where we would state our preferred profession, dress accordingly and sing in a round. So I would introduce the song, act my part and stand back allowing the next star to do his bit before joining in and so on.

It sounds crap but ten people in a line singing and gesticulating away raised the roof.

The professions by the way were me an undertaker having my balls cut off by the tailor who in turn was barged into by a very Peter Sellers Indian bus conductor.

A camp dance instructor was run over by an Irish driving instructor whilst the golfer swung his huge number three wood over all our heads. I'm afraid I have used this same act unashamedly in many bars, functions and village halls ever since!

Joff the doctor and me the cop crossing the line

Crossing the line was always a big party. We would carefully select our victims, young girls and small thick 'yarpie' men, as it wouldn't do to take the piss out of large ones. As the old saying goes the bigger they are the harder they hit you! A court was set up for the crossing the line ceremony next to the pool where I as policeman would drag the suitably sozzled accused.

The judge would read out their crimes, usually in

the case of woman something like, 'you were found wearing nothing but one thousand beads, beads of perspiration'. To which the baying crowds would howl guilty.

The sentence would then be passed involving brother Joff dressed up as a highly suspect doctor doing things with eggs tucked down bikini bottoms and a large mallet. I had the honour of firmly holding the struggling victims down, a pleasant and revealing task as I recall.

The prisoner was then flung into the swimming pool to join a purser dressed as a bear.

He had a particularly nasty can of dye tucked in his costume which turned the pool a disgusting shade of brown.

The male victims were shrouded in a sheet and laid on the operating table. Joff then proceeded to operate using large theatrical saws and tongs and suitable amounts of a bright red liquid for gore! From the victim's genital area he would pull a long very large sausage and flatten it with the mallet before cutting it off with the saw, a touch of ritual tribal circumcision comes to mind. The soaking wet prisoners were awarded a certificate then liberally doused with Castle lager for being such good sports.

I met a girl in Port Elizabeth called Barbara who I named Bunny for short. Two reasons really, one she never stopped talking and two she went like a fucking rabbit. After we had finished our horizontal activity, I'm not sure she didn't talk all the way through that either, even with her mouth full, we would lunch on the beach then back to the boat. She would be still nattering away as I closed the cabin door. Five days later after I had been up to Durban and back there would be a knock on the door, in she would come, undress and continued the same conversation.

Now the girls in PE were desperate to escape the tiny township and saw marrying an officer as a way to escape. It brings back the Officer and a Gentleman film theme again, you remember I thought I looked like Richard Gere.

Perks of the job!

Anyway on one trip after docking in Port Elizabeth the cabin door received its usual knock at seven a.m. Bunnies voice announced, 'Robin I'm with child'. 'Bring it in then' I said, not amused that she was bringing an infant to my room, 'no man I'm pregnant' she answered. Obviously desperate to escape the tiny township and hoping to secure my hand in marriage she had ceased contraception. Well not to be callous I thought bang goes my bang and our usual boozy lunch in a local hotel. Realising things were not going to plan she took me to a large house on the outskirts of town, told me she was going to see her auntie and disappeared. Coming out some time later, very pale and in tears she told me everything was okay now, feeling nauseous I remembered P.E was the abortion town of South Africa and seeing my auntie was the euphemism the girls used.

Not surprising Bunny curtailed her visits, looking for another less extreme way to escape perhaps. I was not happy about that episode, I would have expected to be at least consulted and the situation discussed before such a radical solution was used.

Six weeks later, tired, tanned and the recipient of far too much alcohol we were in sight of Southampton with only the dregs party to attend. Each trip an officer's cabin was selected for the final bash. After your watch, with tearful girlfriend in tow, clutching the remnants of your own cabin's booze, hence the term dregs, we would drink in the arrival of our homeport. Sometimes the party would continue long after docking especially when Father was involved.

The ten days shore leave passed in a flash, just long enough to bore my friends rigid, go to a poster shop, music emporium and John Collier tailors who had, as the natty line said, the window to watch. Well sod all was going on in the window so I went on in to get properly rigged out. Black flares, velvet bow tie and cummerbund, the biggest kipper tie in the world and a dress shirt that had so many frills it would take a month to iron.

I was now one of the cool dudes. After careful consideration I bought the Easy Rider poster, some 'yachty' ones and my masterstroke Desiderata. The one that goes, no less than the moon and the sun you have a right to be here etc, I'll tell you how it became the number one tool in my seduction routine later. Perhaps tool wasn't such a good word to use.

I bought the biggest portable Hi Fi, as they were then known, Ghetto Blaster in today's parlance that would fit in my cabin along with a selection of tapes. Beach Boys to get the party going, Beatles for a singsong, Cat Stevens if she was a bit mystical and a number of 'smoochy' ones Diana Ross, Barry White, you know the types.

Armed with my action kit I set up my cabin, red shades on the light and listen to this, a dimmer actuated from the bed! I checked on the duty list and saw two new names under day worker and mine as 'genny' man on the eight to twelve watch responsible for running the giant generators that powered the ship. No more posing round deck and no more nights off for me. Neil Clang had also been promoted down below I noted with a sigh of satisfaction.

Along the corridor came the big ugly engineer, 'got you then' he said, 'time to do proper engineering now and no more pissing around doing shows with the poofter pursers' and went off laughing.

I don't suppose he would laugh if he knew his nickname was Boris, as he was a dead ringer for Boris Karloff. I became very aware of his Quasimodo looks the next day whilst working up in the top of the boiler room with him.

We had a leak in a steam pipe so he was crawling through from one direction and me the other. You remember when you were kids a good way to frighten your smaller brother was to creep into his darkened bedroom holding a lit torch under your chin and pulling a face. Well I came round a bend in the pipe to meet Boris with an inspection lamp illuminating his distorted features. Do you know how fast you can back out of a high-pressure steam pipe? Fucking fast, I can tell you.

Life down below was a hot cacophony of diesels

thumping, turbines whining, steam hissing and everything very, very oily. Four-hour watches steamed the life out of you. We stood under so called cooling fans, which blew hot air at you as you drank iced water and chewed salt tablets. Our freezer man came up with the bright idea of lashing blocks of ice on top of our heads with rags and letting them cool you as they melted. We were soft in the head to trust him and suffered memory lapses from freezing our alcohol soaked brains.

Steam was the lifeblood of the ship so when we had all too frequent problems with the boilers the genny man had to take very swift action to stop a black out. We had two steam turbine generators on line at sea with a standby diesel for emergencies. If a boiler threw a wobbler the steam 'genny's' would start to slow and the lights dim. I would have to run to the air start and blast the diesel into life then scramble to the main platform and watch the volt and amp meters climb with the engine speed until with a clash of sparks you could pull shut the main breakers.

On top of each cylinder open indicator valves would emit sheets of flames sounding like gunfire until you could shut them off, it certainly got the adrenaline going. Then the hard work would start, trying to repair the problem in the boiler room. We would all have to turn to for as long as it took to put the boiler back on line. Sometimes idiot passengers would break into the top of the funnel and shut a steam valve, they must have had a death wish.

Watch keeping required a different game plan to day work on the social scene, the eight to twelve watch had its positive and negatives. The downside was working at night when all the entertainment was on, fortunately the disco shut at one a.m. giving just enough time to hand over your watch, dash up top, speed shower, pull on your uniform and make the disco for a few last drinks.

The Chinese laundry made a wonderful job of starching your whites but it took all your strength to force your arms and legs into them. A handy tip for ultra quick donning of uniform was to bend them a little thus breaking the starch then have a practise run before going on watch. If you forgot you arrived on deck crackling and could only walk sideways looking like a refugee from a Lowry painting or a very well dressed crab.

At midday when you came off watch a similar system was used only shorts were easier to pull on. A stroll down to the tourist pool bar and a quick pre lunch mingle would usually result in a late night assignation in the disco.

The ships official entertainment closed at one in the morning allowing the officers to play their trump card over the male passengers. 'It's too early for bed' we would say, 'one of the guys is having a party, loads of other girls, would you like to go'? This is where knowledge of the ships stairs and alleyways came in as you sneaked the girls up top.

By previous arrangement one of the guys would be having drinks so we would cram into his cabin, smoke and drink until the host called time when stage two came in, 'would you care for a night cap'? A quick dash to your cabin, music on, lights dimmed, drinks poured who could ask for anything more!

So as not to think I was presumptive I would sit on the day couch allowing my companion to perch on the main bed in perfect safety. That night or maybe the next she would look up and see my Desiderata poster blue tacked to the deck head. To read it you had to lie down, I rest my case.

Later as the dawn crept over the horizon the girls

would appear out of various officers cabins and sneak back down over the decks to their cabins passing the ship's crew washing down the decks. As most were still dolled up in party dresses and high heels the disgruntled crew would normally mutter something about those lucky fucking officers!

I met a girl one day by the tourist pool and arranged to meet her later explaining that I was on watch until midnight. Struggling to pull on my whites I ran down to the disco still buttoning up the top. The reason for my haste was because the off watch officers had all evening to lure any girl back to their cabins, the game was highly competitive.

All was well and she was there, admittedly with some other no hopers that we managed to quickly throw off.

I ran the late night party line, which she went for, and later we were back in my cabin drinking and talking. Sensing a slow approach was applicable at five am I escorted her intact back down to her deck arranging to meet by the pool at lunchtime.

Dressed in my best whites with purple engineer's epaulettes I found her sitting by the pool with an elderly couple who turned out to be her parents. The father did not look happy. 'Now then young man, what the bloody hell do you think you were doing keeping daughter out t 'five int' morning'.

Please excuse the James Herriot speak but the gentleman was obviously from the northern part of our fair country. 'I've a good mind to take belt to you', 'now then Jack, said t wife don't take on so'. I thought here we go reported to the top brass again, it's a dismissal or banning off decks at least. He carried on in the same theme for a while before spotting my epaulets.

Pausing in his tirade he asked, 'are you an engineer'? When I replied with an affirmative he rounded on his daughter. 'You never said he was an engineer, I thought you wer't wit one of them stuck up deck 'prissies' this puts a different perspective on't matter'. It appeared he was an ex Naval engineer with no love of Johnny deck officers. He then told his daughter to buy me a drink and grilled me for an hour about the ships systems. I suggested that maybe he would like to see them for himself and arranged to meet outside the engine room door at eight.

That evening I took him around the whole engine room, even fitting him out in a boiler suit. At the end of the tour once more back on deck he shook my hand and thanked me. 'by t' way if you want to see daughter its fine by me, I can trust a fellow engineer, don't mind what time she gets in neither' and walked off down the corridor.

That night I stood in the disco trying to find the daughter. Last night she wore trousers and a polo necked top with her hair tied up and glasses. There was a light touch on my arm and turning I saw a completely different girl. Tonight she was wearing a tiny mini skirt and a low necked top that left little to the imagination.

'Father loved his visit, why don't we go straight to your cabin' she said. As I poured our drinks I turned to see her shake her hair down and remove her glasses just like those sexy secretaries in the TV adverts. She went back very early that morning and every morning after for the rest of the trip. The Mum and Dad were good fun too buying me many drinks and telling me tales of his adventures on the high seas.

One night on watch, having a well earned brew, I was leaning back on my chair up against the breaker panel watching the genny's thundering away. There was a loud bang as a genny tripped out and then all went black. I had been smacked on the back of my head by one of the breaker handles. My relief thought I was pissed so left me there to be discovered by an irate second engineer. It was only when I showed them the huge bruise on my neck that I was pardoned, yet another near miss I thought.

I realised that Boris was not such a bad guy and to boot was extremely resourceful. In Durban we had a major repair on one of the huge main boilers. It took twenty-four hours to cool down a boiler and as we only had three days to fix the dammed things we took shortcuts. The shortcut being to insert the lightest, smallest junior engineer through a boiler manhole and though it's hard to believe now, at that time it was me.

Wriggling through the tiny aperture I found myself in the furnace which by the light of the inspection lamp glowed with luminescent colours of burnt carbon, brilliant greens and vivid reds all shimmering in the boiling temperature.

'Stop fucking about looking at the pretty colours' shouted Boris through the hatch, 'and by the way did you know your shoes are on fire'. Doing the engine room boot soft-shoe shuffle I searched for the tell tale cracks in the furnace walls. When I had finished I found that I had expanded with the heat and couldn't get out. Being acutely claustrophobic this was not a good thing, help! There was I gently broiling inside the boiler with smouldering feet and my fellow crew outside wondering how to get me out.

It was Boris who came up with the solution. They soaked some engine room sacks with water from a fire hose and pushed them through the manhole, wrap yourself in those and hold the hose over you Boris shouted. Eventually I cooled down enough to squeeze through the door to freedom very relieved and several pounds lighter.

Banned off Deck

Sometimes we had so called entertainers singing for their suppers on the down coast trip. One couple who boarded in Durban were fairly typical, he played passengers requests on the piano and she sang badly. Most nights he accepted a drink per request, which made his later songs fairly indeterminate, and she appeared to be making a survey of officer's cabins.

One quiet night I appeared to be top of her list so whilst entertaining her in my cabin listening to what an arsehole her partner was there came a knock on the door. Arthur's my stewards voice was full of urgency, 'Robin' he shouted 'if you're busy get her out the porthole the top brass are coming with her old man leading the way'.

With a whirr of the porthole handles madam was out on the deck closely followed by a dress, various bits of 'twangy' gear, shoes and an ashtray full of lipstick stained fags. Fanning the cabin with a towel and liberally spraying Brute aftershave I jumped back into bed and feigned sleep.

Moments later there was a commotion in the alleyway along the lines of let me at him and a pounding on the door. When I swung the door open there stood the first officer with two burly Masters at Arms sitting on an extremely drunk not to say irate pianist! Stifling a yawn I enquired how I could be of assistance. The Mate looked in and said 'she's not here sir', gave me a meaningful look and ushered the still protesting drunk away. Whew I thought and gave myself a glance in the mirror, covered in lipstick I was not a pretty sight.

Jimmy and Arthur came scurrying around for some very well deserved beers and gave me the low down. Apparently when the bar shut the pissed pianist starting creating and said his girlfriend had gone off with an officer named Tickner. Joff's cabin was nearest so he received the first visit, fortunately as he explained later he was not entertaining so when the lynching party made off he rang Arthur to warn me. Thank heavens for elder brothers yet again!

The top brass were not fooled, so at another rather difficult meeting I was banned off decks and the name went into the little black book yet again. The sentence meant I wasn't allowed onto the tourist decks or take part in any form of entertaining. This wasn't as bad as it sounds. Due to my pouring drinks down the master at arms necks on every opportunity meant that they not only turned a blind eye to parties in my cabin they even escorted my current beau up top whilst I was on watch.

All things come to pass and I met a lady on the down coast trip to Cape Town, Siobhan was her name and she truly took my breath away. Very young tall and elegant I promised her I would take her out for the meal of a lifetime in the windy city. Fate had some cards to play however, it was my night on board when we docked which meant no night of passion, instead I was in charge of the engine room.

At about midnight on my rounds I found a drunken donkey man had jammed a metal rod in the auxiliary boiler. Hoping to free it I was wrestling away trying to remove the dammed thing when he sloped off.

There was an almighty roar and a sheet of flame engulfed me setting my boiler suit on fire. The prat had opened the wrong valve and back pressurised the boiler making it into a giant flame-thrower. Rolling about the engine room plates looking like St Joan it was fortunate some shore side workers threw some sacks over me and smothered the flames. They picked me up and rushed me to the ship's doctor.

Now Doctor John was as queer as a coot and had

promised to get my pants off for some time but there is a time and a place! He put me into a salt water bath and switched the air on, it was I supposed an early version of a Jacuzzi but it worked. My boiler suit had burned itself into my skin and as for my 'Marks and Sparks's' nylon pants well they had moulded themselves to my genitals.

The salt water did its thing and Dr John was able to pull most of my clothes off with tweezers accompanied by much shouting from myself. Morphine was injected and a bed in the ship's hospital was my lot complete with subdued lighting.

Brother Joff staggered back to the ship later after a night on the town to find a note saying I had been blown up and was in the hospital. It must have looked like the suicide scene from M.A.S.H. when he lurched in. That morphine is a bloody good drug, I woke up in the morning and remembered I was taking Siobhan out for the day, so looking a little like an extra from the curse of the mummy I got dressed and walked off the ship into the arms of my beloved.

We did have that great meal, perhaps a little marred by me passing out mid course. She even managed to sneak me back on the ship undetected much to the confusion of the medical staff that had been searching high and low for me.

Due to Dr John's ministrations and the magic salt water bubble bath I was unscarred and enjoyed the hospitality of Union Castle as a passenger for the trip back. To stop Mum worrying Joff had sent a telegram saying I had been slightly singed.

I paid off the ambulance at the bottom of our road and walked stiffly home into the arms of my family. When I showed Mom my chest she fainted under the kitchen table, I had forgotten they had painted me with bright red iodine!

Big hearted as ever the company bought me a new boiler suit and engine room boots, the nylon knickers are on exhibition at the Tate gallery alongside the sheep in formaldehyde!

An Officer and a Gentleman

Cupid's arrow had found its mark, for the next two trips I wished the time away until I saw Siobhan in Durban. I had some leave due so I talked to her about coming out on the Windsor, having a holiday in Durban with her and then going back on my new ship the Pendennis Castle. A great idea I thought but shades of an Officer and a Gentleman were looming again.

Dad was bank manager at Basildon new town by this time with a glass office looking over the high street with views of Essex girls in all their majesty. I only know one clean Essex girl joke, what's the difference between an Essex girl and a supermarket trolley? A supermarket trolley has a mind of its own!

Anyway as I was going to South Africa for three months he advised me to get my teeth looked at. Strange advice you might think but our childhood toothpaste had consisted of a pink paste in a round tin with no effect on tooth decay but you could do great rabies impersonations. I had two teeth extracted and four fillings before ambling round to his bank. In his office doing a Dudley Moore impersonation the bit where he tries to drink coffee with numbed lips, I accepted a medicinal whisky whilst counting my bank rate foreign currency.

With swollen gums and blood leaking from my mouth I drove to Croydon for a goodbye meal with my girlfriend. Horrified and probably quite glad to get rid of me she fed me soup and a glass of wine.

I took my leave at midnight and set off for my ship. This was long before the M3 so I drove back up to London and sped along the embankment. I saw a flashing blue light behind me so dutifully pulled over. Now Dad had always said if you're stopped by the police always get out of the car and walk towards them to show you're sober. Great advices as long as you're not wearing a sleeping bag.

Let me explain. Joff and I shared a MGB roadster so as I was going to South Africa I had my surfboard in the passenger seat, but to get it in I had to have the roof down. So what I hear you say, well it was December and it was snowing but to add to the situation the cars fuel pump was playing up. The solution to this mechanical problem was to hang out of the door and twat it with a hammer whilst still underway.

In hindsight a sports car with its lid down in December, snowing, one o'clock in the morning wearing a bobble hat, I had forgotten that bit, well it was cold, driver leaning out the door with a hammer accompanied by a surfboard does make a fairly arresting sight. Remembering Dads advice I got out of the car and fell straight over, sleeping bags keep you warm but are very hard to walk in. Regaining my composure I hopped up to the police car like a late entry in a school sack race and bade good evening to the slightly confused police officers. Well I tried to speak but due to my still numb gums I made little sense.

A pretty green colour shone from their breathalyser and after they had stopped laughing I was invited to accompany them to their Bow Street police station. The sight of one of the boys in blue driving the MG through the snow is a sight I will never forget. Apparently the dentist's drugs and the alcohol had put me over the limit. Explaining I had to join my ship by ten in the morning they kindly banged me up for the night.

At three in the morning I had to ring the parents to send my driving documents to the forces of law, good old Dad took it in his stride but I could hear Mom in the background moaning about what the neighbours were going to say about her son spending a night in prison.

At six am, despite a still positive breathalyser the boys sent me on my way to Southampton and to the arms of my beloved in Durban.

Just like that bloody Richard Gere film Siobhan was happy with me as an officer and a gentleman but only for three days a trip and not as a poor holiday maker! After two days she made it clear she had her own life and I clearly was not part of it. Feeling a right prat I sadly took my leave and took the sailors remedy, and got pissed. Staggering back along Durban's seafront I chanced upon two burly 'yarpies' giving a slightly shabby girl a hard time. Pulling myself up to my full five foot seven and a half foot height I told them to piss off. Obviously scared that I was going to puke on them they concurred and left me to drive erratically home accompanied by the girl.

She desperately needed a bath and clean clothes so I left her soaking whilst I as a true gentleman passed out in my bed. Waking up in the morning I found her snuggled up next to me which slightly took the edge off being dumped the day before. We had a great week before sending her back to Johannesburg leaving me with time on my hands, where to go and what to do ?

I resorted again to the sailors remedy but this time met a great character named John in a bar on Durban's seafront. Early next morning a stone against my window woke me to find John at my doorstep, bags packed ready for our next adventure!

I had apparently organised to drive with John down the 'garden route' all the way to Cape Town. This road follows the coast through stunning scenery and is now one of the must do's of a South African holiday. Back in those days you had to drive through several African townships where law and order had yet to be established. Burnt out wrecks of cars stood as a testimony of how rough things were. A favourite trick was to send cute little kids out on the road selling maize or bloody wooden elephants. When the driver stopped several large men would jump out from behind bushes to attack and rob the cars occupants.

Mindful of this John spent the whole trip clutching the car jack in his hands waving it threateningly at any pedestrian. I thought this was a bit over the top as he started his antics in the middle of Durban high street.

With my trusty surfboard lashed to the roof we sped down the coast stopping to surf at Jeffries bay and other notable surfing beaches. Rounding a bend we happened upon two girls hitching and well I never one was an Aussie the other a Kiwi. We spent a convivial two weeks lazily exploring the delights of the coast route and the girls before finally driving into Cape Town.

I forgot to mention John was more than a little fond of the amber nectar. One day after imbibing several gallons of lager we lashed ourselves together with the car towrope and climbed the main high street of Port Elizabeth. We made our base camp at Woolworth's, had some purely medicinal drinks and due to the lack of oxygen outside the chemist fell into a heap much to the surprise of the Saturday shoppers. All this on a horizontal surface without the aid of pitons or Sherpa's!

Due to a lack of funds we stayed in the cheapest hotel, more a shack really, in a down town area of Cape Town. In the middle of the night after drinking the town dry I awoke to the sound of gunfire to see John leaning out of the window aiming his finger at the street battle below. Bullets whistling off the window frame didn't faze him. Fool hardy or just plain pissed he was certainly an experience and sadly when we parted I never saw him again.

So Cape Town, the windy city what should I do? As I pondered looking out over Table Bay I saw the familiar sight of a Union Castle liner docking. Driving to the docks I realised it was the Pendennis Castle with brother Joff on board. After another convivial night spent with Joff in the bars of Cape Town I woke with a creaking head and discovered I had bet I could beat the ship up coast to Durban in my car. An easy task one would think as cars can do lots of MPH and ships do a lot less. Top Gear contests similar to the Hampster and James May taking on Clarkson come to mind but I had not counted on fuel sanctions. Garages were only open at set times and not at weekends. Still a bet is a bet so early next morning as the ship set sail I roared off into the hinterland surfboard on roof and provisions in boot.

After a few hours I picked up a sailor, as you do, hitching. One hundred miles later the 'yarpy' prat realised he had left his kit bag by the roadside and asked to return, so of course I turned back, did I hell. I turfed the bastard out and conscience clear, sped on my way. I slept in the car that night in the middle of the veldt. I don't know what a veldt is but I've slept in one, and at dawn, foot hard down I was back on the road.

Crossing a dusty plain with a couple of native huts, a giraffe and one tree in the distance I saw the unmistakable uniform of the South African police. He was about one hundred miles away standing in the middle of the road with one arm outstretched in the familiar you're nicked my son pose. When I eventually reached him, I got out of the car as per Dads instructions, and was greeted with a torrent of Afrikaans. Apparently I was speeding and leading me behind the one tree he showed me a radar trap. 'You were doing over one hundred and fifty kilometres an hour' he shouted. Thinking quickly, knowing these jerks can fine you on the spot or if black, shoot you, I noted his name on his shiny badge. 'Mr Van Da Merwe', I said 'don't you remember me'? 'I was third engineer on the Union Castle ship you had your holiday on'.

Now most South Africans at some time went up or down coast on our ships so it wasn't such a long shot. A look of confusion creased his Neanderthal forehead, 'you and your wife were such wonderful dancers and didn't you do well at the bingo'. That clinched it. With a careful look round at the miles of bugger all he ripped up the speeding ticket and wished me on my way adding he had a fellow officer in another township on the way but he would tip him the wink. Barrelling through the little village a couple of hours later another cop with thumb raised disappeared into my cloud of dust as I roared through.

I slept that night again in the car parked outside a village hut with a crudely painted sign hanging from it announcing butcher. Waking late I found myself surrounded by a sea of curious faces. Discretion being the better part of valour I decided to drive off toot sweet. Unfortunately the battery disagreed so I stayed put. I explained my problem to a large native wearing a blood stained apron who disappeared into the hut and reappeared with a menacing cleaver. This is it I thought, Englishman kebab for the village dinner tonight. Lifting my bonnet he used the cleaver as a makeshift screwdriver and removed the battery. Whilst charging it we had breakfast with his family, antelope omelette as I recall before sending me on my way, battery and spirits recharged.

I lost my bet, the Pendennis had docked a day before I sleepily bowled into Durban. Returning my trusty hire car I walked up the gangplank to join my new ship.

The Pendennis was older than the Windsor but in my opinion was a prettier ship. Nicknamed the penis castle it was a favourite with young South Africans escaping the African continent on their voyage of discovery to Europe.

Due to my extended time away from England's shores and Joff's leaving the ship we arranged for dad to meet us in Southampton to pick us and our excessive luggage including my surfboard, up.

It was my turn to host the dregs party and also unfortunately to shut down the engine room after docking.

The Pendennis Castle

The party was in full swing as we berthed in Southampton. After several hours shutting down the boilers I made my weary way back to my cabin. I could hear hooting and a hollering from down the alleyway and after forcing my way into my still packed cabin I found father drunk as a lord regaling the throng with war time stories, much like dear old 'Uncle Albert' from only 'Fools and Horses'. Eventually Joff and I prised dad away from the ship, threw him into the boot of the car and drove home.

After the usual homecoming celebrations taking several hours Mum asked where Dad was. We found him still in the boot with a happy smile curled up with the spare wheel surrounded by our luggage.

The Pendennis castle was another two class ship so more fine dining in first class and more chasing down to the tourist class after watch to sample the joys of young South African womanhood.

One early morning enjoying a post watch beer our team hatched a new strategy to fill the twelve to four graveyard watch. The second engineer was a bit of a food gourmet so we decided to open an engine room restaurant for the sole use of our ladies. Invitations were issued to our beau's for Friday night and a menu printed. Tomato soup followed by steak, steamed vegetables and baked potato with whatever was left in the galley for desert. The fridge man who had the keys to the cold room nicked the main ingredients, knives and forks were obtained from the first class saloon as were the tablecloth, napkins and condiments. All these were hidden behind an instrument panel in the genny flat along with some purloined pots and pans from the galley. A way into the engine room and escape route for the ladies was planned along with an alarm system in case of intruders. The whole plan began to resemble an episode from Colditz!

On the due day each member of the watch took his or her allocated foodstuffs and started cooking. In the 'genny' room I wrapped the potatoes in silver foil and cooked them on one of the steam genny's whilst warming the soup on a condenser. In the boiler room the third engineer was flash frying the steaks in a pan balanced on a furnace door. The veggies were quietly simmering on the main turbines as the fridge man laid the table, a board resting on a compressor, before meeting the girls. We changed into clean white boiler suits with bow ties and poured the chilled white wine. The girls, entering into the spirit of the evening, well morning really as it was two am, arrived wearing evening dresses and clutching fancy handbags. The effect was slightly marred by the wearing of sensible footwear, as stilettos tend to slip on oily engine room floors. We enjoyed a convivial meal surrounded by whirring turbines, roaring boilers and the occasional alarm before sending the girls on their way back to our cabins. The whole kit and caboodle was then packed away, hidden and normal service resumed.

The restaurant opened three more nights before the chief engineer with a keen sense of smell wondered why his engine room instead of smelling of oil bore odours of garlic and fried onions. 'Great scam' he told us 'but before one of your guests gets pissed and falls into the bilge you had better shut your restaurant and get all those bloody pots and pans out of the control panel and back to the galley before the purser rumbles you'!

You tend to forget that chiefs were once junior engineers and got up to similar high japes.

As a side thought on a similar vein of we were all young once, there is a great sailor named Mick who ran a sailing school in Burnham on Crouch from an old Second World War torpedo boat. At a sailing club dinner many moons ago we were on the passing the port stage, men dressed in blazers and ties and the ladies done up in long dresses. Mick in his cups decided to run down the table scattering wine bottles, glasses and plates in his wake leaping over the commodore before disappearing up the sea wall.

Mick was elected commodore of the club this year!

I had several happy trips on the Pendennis, the Desiderada poster was still working its magic on the deck head above my bed but the next conquest marked the beginning of a slight feeling of dissatisfaction with the Union Castle bus run.

Surveying the passengers at the Captains Cocktail

party big Andy the third mate and I were picked up by a mother and daughter. Obviously old hands they dispensed with the niceties and invited themselves up to our cabins. Andy was dragged onto the main bed by the mother whilst the daughter threw me on the day bed and started tugging at my uniform trousers. Now I'm not a prude but the last time I slept with a daughter with her mother watching she 'baaaaad'! Anyway I tried to get back to my own cabin but she would have none of it. The next night the same pair found us and the same happened only they swapped partners! Deciding they were a little strange we tried to avoid them but the following lunchtime accompanied by an elderly man they cornered us in the pool bar. 'Let me buy you a drink' the old chap said 'as a thank you for entertaining my wife and daughter, I've been seasick since we left Southampton'. We avoided that trio like a plague for the rest of the trip! One does have principles you know.

One of the big don'ts was never enter a passenger cabin by yourself a heinous crime and punishable by banning off deck or dismissal. It also kept you safe from some of the strange requests that certain ladies made. As day work engineer I was once summoned to fix a ladies shower to find her in it and wanting a golden shower. I'll say no more.

Late one night, two elderly female passengers rushed up to me jabbering that they had seen a face at the porthole, a tad unlikely as they were in tourist class in a cabin that looked straight out to sea. Grabbing a fellow officer we looked into their cabin to make sure it wasn't piled high with empty gin bottles before reporting the situation to the bridge.

The ship was slowed as a cabin search was conducted and sure enough one passenger was missing .On his bed was a letter wishing the world goodbye obviously written before leaping over the side and scaring the two old biddies on his way down.

With searchlights sweeping the sea we slowly went back until one eagle eyed lookout spotted something floating in the water. A ships lifeboat was launched, as the ship lay gently rolling on the swell, and puttered its way towards the jumper. The passengers thought this was all part of the ships entertainment and lined the rails cheering. Sadly there is no happy ending. As the lifeboat got close to the guy he rolled over and sank, a sombre crew made its way back to the ship as we doused the lights and went on our way.

SA Vaal in Cape Town

The company liked to move its officers around the fleet to gain experience of different systems so with another stripe on my shoulder I joined the SA Vaal painted in the livery of SAF Marine but run and staffed by Union Castle. She was the newest ship of the line and unlike the others was one class. For the well heeled there were luxury suites and smaller cabins for the usual crowd of young South Africans going overseas as they put it.

When I was young I saw Swiss Family Robinson at the local fleapit and fell in love with its star, Hayley Mills. A rumour went round the Vaal that she was joining the ship in Cape Town for the trip home. I was happily swimming around the pool minding my own business one afternoon when I bumped into someone. Turning around I came face to face with the film star. I say face to face but actually it was face to feet as for some stupid reason I bowed low nearly drowning myself!

Hayley was travelling with her husband the film producer Roy Boulting, her son, and a nanny. In the fullness of time I got to know her nanny in the biblical sense. She would put the child to bed in the suite next to his parents before sliding away to my cabin. One evening I was summoned to meet Roy Boulting in the library, with a slight feeling of déjà vu I shook hands and asked how I could help him. 'Tell the bloody nanny to lock the cabin door when she comes down to shag you, the little lad keeps letting himself into our cabin at god knows what time and waking us up'! After apologising we moved onto safer ground.

'I want to have a cocktail party for the officers, who do the real work on this ship ' he said, 'like the engineers and mates not the bloody chief radio officer'.

I proposed the idea to the first engineer whose day cabin like most senior officers was often used for such parties. True to his word invitations were issued to the watch keepers and on the night Roy stood at the cabin door and barred all the top brass who tried to gate crash. I got to know the Boulting's a bit on the trip and the nanny quite a lot so when the chief engineer escorted them down to the engine room Hayley came over to me and watched as we manoeuvred the ship into port. Chest filled with pride I span them giant silver wheels with my hero standing beside me much to the chagrin of the chief.

I was now a watch keeper in the main turbine room dominated by the giant control panel full of gauges the one that had so frightened me on my first visit below just a few short years ago. Every watch you had to fill in a giant logbook with steam pressures, fuel consumption and a host of other data the most important being the engine revolutions. The two turbines had to be kept at the same speed so the rev counters should be equal, the throttles were supposed to be monitored constantly and adjusted accordingly.

One watch after a rather energetic night I must have dozed off, as when I awoke the rev counters were way different. Radical action was needed to sort this out before the chief came down on his rounds. The simplest way was to slow one engine and speed up the other. Five minutes later a call from the bridge asked me what the bloody hell was going on as the ship was going around in circles! I got my own back as the deck officer who bollocked me fell asleep on his watch the next night as we sailed from Port Elizabeth to Cape Town. There is a strong current running down the coast, which enabled us to run at slow speed with only two boilers fired up thus saving fuel.

This particular night with the third mate dozing happily on the bridge the usual request to slow right down to enter Cape Town at first light never came.

Eventually a panic stricken voice from the bridge begged me to slow down as quick as possible as we were just passing Table Mountain. We apparently whizzed around Table Bay several times before I got the ship down to manoeuvring speed, throwing passengers out of their beds and confusing the hell out of Nelson Mandela imprisoned on Robin Island. Not true but a nice thought!

All communications from the bridge came to the main engine room platform, some stranger than others. One day the mate asked me to level the ship as the cricket mad captain wanted to play a game of deck cricket. Pumping oil from one side of the ship to the other would bring the ship upright so off I went with my wheel spanner, opened the valves and started the oil pump. Something must have distracted me as the phone jumped off its cradle and an irate Captain informed me he wanted to play cricket not take up mountain climbing. I had over compensated a trifle, the ship was now listing heavily the other way, whoops!

On another occasion we were sailing through the Bay of Biscay homeward bound towards the English winter so the sea water temperature was beginning to drop in the first class pool. The message from the bridge was to crack some steam on and make the pool warmer. Again I was distracted to be told by the jangling phone that there was steam coming off the pool, an elderly dowager had scorched herself and some joker had thrown some tea bags into the pool making it into a giant teapot. No sense of humour these deck officers.

We used chemicals to flush through the ships systems, which sometimes had an alarming effect on any sea creatures, trapped in the strainers. One night the genny man found a giant fluorescent crab in the sea suction so he carefully laid it in the main engine logbook and gently closed the cover. Hiding behind a pump we watched the third engineer casually open the book then with a scream slam it shut again. It took the whole watch for him to remove the crab-splattered pages and laboriously re enter all the readings.

My time on passenger ships was running out, I felt that we were on an extended bus route there must be more to see then Cape Town, Port Elizabeth, East London and even Durban was getting to lose its appeal. I had been banned off decks yet again, for having my Durban girlfriend stay on board for three days so the ships little black book had another Tickner entry in it.

I had also met Sally, on the previous trip, who was later to become my first wife and I was missing her.

The crunch came when I was found in the first class pool early one morning sleeping on a steamer chair. Not such a bad crime I hear you say, unfortunately I was naked and so was my female companion and the two empty bottles of bubbly was deemed as a health hazard by the over zealous and probably over jealous master at arms who found me.

I was summoned by the Captain who read me the riot act, banned me off decks and requested the company remove me from passenger ships for good and for me to get my just deserts at head office.

Back in Southampton I packed my bags for the last time and walked off the ship with a mixture of sadness tinged with anticipation of new and exciting destinations.

As I walked into the companies London head office the typing pool girls were clapping. After receiving the mandatory bollocking and my 'Dishonourable Discharge' stamp in my seaman's book the engineering superintendent said with a twinkle in his eye that 'I would now be sailing on Clan Line cargo ships so the female passengers would in future be safe' and gave me a beer. 'Why were the girls clapping when I came in I asked'? 'Well to liven up their days', he admitted, 'copies of the little black ships disciplinary book would be passed around, they have been following your antics for some time'.

So my 'passy' days were over and after a long leave to get to know Sally I was summoned to join the Clan Graham as fourth engineer and guess where it was going, sodding South Africa!

Clan Boats

Before setting off once more on my travels Sally decided that I should meet her parents who lived in Ryton Eleven towns in Shropshire. They were more lord and lady of the manor in an eccentric sort of way living in a huge tumble down house in the middle of the countryside. It was winter so they had a huge fire burning in an inglenook fireplace, so big it had seats in the hearth. They had managed a rubber plantation in Malaysia where Sally had been brought up. Supping a sizeable gin and tonic her mother piped up. 'Remember old Jock the engineer the one who got his cock shot off', I was on home ground here they were barking mad just like my parents. I moved Sally in with Richards's girlfriend Tessa in Hutton Essex and professing undying love disappeared off to sea.

Back I went to my old haunts knowing that when the lights of Cape Town twinkled in the dark African sky I would once again be enthralled with this wonderful continent.

The company were playing jokes with me. The next ship I joined as Fourth engineer was the oldest in the fleet the Clan McIlwraith. She had sailed with twelve passengers in the old days, living in luxury wood panelled cabins, tramping around the world with no set itinerary but often round Africa and back through the Suez Canal.

After several years on a steam ship going back to diesel main engines was a culture shock especially when it turned out to be a Doxford. Picture this if you can. Now most of us can grasp the rudiments of a car engine, one piston per cylinder with a spark plug, carburettor, con rods and a flywheel, but the Doxford had two pistons per cylinder. Two connecting rods with two fuel injectors blasting atomised diesel between the two opposed pistons with a normal arrangement downwards and some sort of overhead con rod and trunnion gear transferring the thrust to the main crank.

That's about as much technical nonsense as this missive will stand but as the engine farted and moaned with massive metal bits flailing around at about sixty rpm I thought how different to the smooth turbines of my old 'passy' boats. The top speed was only twelve knots flat out so voyages were going to take much longer than the six-week mail run I had got used to. Manoeuvring was interesting with loads of valves and wheels to throw about doing what was known as the 'Doxford dance'.

The ship was fairly antique like a well worn shoe, wallowing her way around tiny off the beaten track ports. Passengers had long since selected planes as their preferred choice of transport so the officers now inhabited their panelled staterooms.

We pulled into Cape Town, powerful tugs pushed us into the dry dock for some hull repairs. As the dock was pumped out a team of convict labourers with long scrapers started cleaning the hull up to their wastes in water. Unfortunately for them a shark was trapped in the dock and was not happy, boy them convicts can swim fast.

The dry dock was a long way from town so one lecherous officer requested a gaggle of Hookers or should that be a shag anyway several giggling black ladies of the night trooped up the gangplank and disappeared into the lads cabins. Now as I have frequently stated I do not partake in this activity so slept peacefully and solitary in my bunk. Waking early I remembered it was Sunday so Captains inspection, best to have a tidy up.

After my morning ablutions I walked back to my cabin and was surprised to hear sounds of great merriment from within. Opening the door I was greeted by the sight of several half naked officers cavorting with the ladies, glancing behind me I saw the Captain beginning his rounds. It must have been quite a sight seeing several woman exiting my cabin arses first through a not very large porthole and I got a bollocking for having an untidy cabin!

After once more enjoying the delights of South Africa we sailed up to Mombasa, scene of the infamous two storey brothel incident but this time I slipped in the main engine and fell into the crankcase.

A knife like pain shot through my back as I lay in the sump with lube oil playing gently over me. The crew pulled me out of the engine and strapping me onto a stretcher I was manhandled out of the engine room into an ambulance and through the streets of 'Mombers' to the hospital.

I was diagnosed as having an abscess on my coccyx, which needed an operation due to a hair growing back into my skin and turning septic. An extremely drunken surgeon took charge and as I was wheeled into the theatre, I had to ask to be put under, as they seemed to have forgotten to administer the anaesthetic! Coming round with a mouth like the bottom of a birdcage I found myself in a general ward surrounded by other mosquito netted patients.

In the morning with an extremely sore arse I was visited by some of the boys from the ship carrying bags that clinked. We had an extremely 'pissy' afternoon out on the veranda watching the sun go down over the ocean. Eventually I was carried back to my mosquito shrouded hospital bed well anaesthetised and tucked up by the boys before they staggered into the dusk.

Two things were memorable about that night, the Israelis stormed the jet at Entebbe and I tried to go to the loo only to be completely entangled in the bloody mossy net, pissed myself and slept on the ward floor!

In the next bed was a Greek steward, gay as a kite who had been trying it on with me. Screens were placed round his bed and a large matron pulling on rubber gloves administered the then current method of pile treatment. His screams as blocks of ice were inserted up his anus were greeted by hoots of derision from the other inhabitants of the ward who had also suffered from his unwelcome advances.

The surgeon's efforts had left a bloody great hole in me, which had to be packed with wadding to allow the skin to re grow from the inside and not heal from the surface. This entailed two beautiful Malaysian nurses pulling the dressings off every day and then repacking me.

They poured some sort of spirit over my arse to clean the plaster off allowing just enough to trickle down and burn my testicles much to my discomfit and their amusement.

After a few more boozy visits from the boys the ship sailed leaving me to the tender mercies of the Mombasa health service. A week later I was deemed fit enough to travel and flew up to Zanzibar, the spice island, to rejoin the ship carrying an inflatable ring to sit on much to my embarrassment and the boys delight.

Zanzibar is a great place, the inhabitants are a mixture of races with unique colouring and fine features. The whole place bustles in the steaming heat and the atmosphere is full of wonderful scents of rich spices and the shouts of the market traders. I liked the place, sore arse and all!

Next stop was Aden in the 'People's Democratic Republic of South Yemen' as written in my dear Mum's handwriting on one of her many letters she laboured over to her seafaring sons. We were banned from going ashore in Aden as a captain's wife from another Clan boat had been shot walking off their gangplank recently. We bunkered and then slipped into the Red Sea where the sun shone fiercely down on the burnished water making it impossible to walk on the ship's decks.

The landscape was a baked dusty brown with no sign of life or vegetation. Towering cliffs lined the banks in places trapping the heat like a furnace as we trudged our way North. The sea temperature rose higher and higher, the sea water pumps were on full speed but still could not cool the main engines so we had to slow the ship down.

I lay on the funnel deck captivated by the scenery, all so different from the muddy banks of Essex. I was reading 'Eagle in the Sky' by Wilbur Smith which was based in the area we were travelling. I could picture the 'Mig' jets soaring through the canyons of the Red Sea and swooping over the mountains, the book came alive in my eyes!

Port Sudan, our next stop was a deserted ex British base. It consisted of dust, sand and a forlorn broken concrete dock with two battered cranes where we deposited a few boxes of cargo. The off watch boys wandered up the road in search of a beer and found a shabby brick building with a broken sign advertising the Port Sudan Polo Club.

Pushing the old door off its hinges, we stepped warily into a billiard room with a table complete with a half finished game, cues still lying on the dusty green baize. The walls were covered with lists of polo captains and tales of their exploits in faded gold writing. All in all it reminded of a land based version of the Marie Celeste. As the bar had been shut for at least fifty years we moved on to a nearby shack that was serving alcohol to slake our thirst, I always wanted to write that.

It was hot, so hot you could hardly breathe, no wonder the Arabs lie down most of the time and as we went north it got drier, dustier even more like the inside of an Aga cooker.

Finally we dropped anchor in the Bay of Eilat right at the top of the Red Sea surrounded by Jordan, Egypt and Israel a rare cauldron of races. We lay gently broiling in the bay waiting our turn to go alongside bored out of our skulls until film day came around.

The good old Bell and Powell projector was dragged up top and a tarpaulin stretched between two derricks. Perhaps my choice of film was not too tactful in our geographical circumstances. The killing of Dudley Krackovitch or something similar was an everyday tale of Jewish folk, which went down a treat with the Israeli gunboat moored on our port side. Our Arab friends on the starboard side were not so pleased. A row of machine gun bullet holes stitched across the screen led to an early interval with a hurried film change to the Jungle Book, deemed safer to all sides!

Aqaba is now a major holiday resort with many hotels and a Mecca for divers but in those days it was a tiny commercial port.

The custom officers used a refrigerated container as their office sided by a taxi rank with a couple of old battered Mercedes.

One of the officers had heard of the ancient sandstone city of Petra, which was a long cab ride away. A hardy band of us hired the taxis and sped off into the desert passing surprised looking Bedouin tribesman on camels tending their sheep. Some Arabs with knackered old donkeys bartered with us to take us down a tiny steep path through the canyon to Petra.

You slip through a narrow entrance in the cliffs into a square surrounded by temples and an amphitheatre hewn out of red sandstone lost for hundreds of years. We spent an incredible few hours wandering around this ancient city completely deserted by any other human souls, a truly memorable afternoon, before getting ripped off by the taxi drivers on the way back to the ship. The city is featured in Spielberg's film Raiders of the Lost Ark.

Me and the boys Petra

One of the benefits of sailing on a general cargo ships was you never knew which ports you would visit. Ships were called tramps and that's what we did, slowly making our way around the world dependant on what cargo we picked up. Trips could last for a year before returning back to a home port in fact triple headers were common.

This was the practise of picking up cargo in Europe taking it to India or Africa then back to the Med then out again and so on until the ship got dizzy! The officers would eventually get flown home whilst the crew would stay until the ship went back to their homeport.

Indian and Pakistan crew were extremely well paid in comparison to their fellow countrymen which is why they tried to stay at sea most of their lives sometimes not seeing their family for years. With the money saved they would buy Singer sewing machines to set up a sweat shop back home for their retirement, old fashioned bicycles were also high on their shopping lists.

Every Friday we tested the ships emergency gear or 'board of trade sports', as it was more commonly known. In port we would lower the lifeboats, start their reluctant diesel engines and putter around the harbour normally in the pouring rain. At sea we would just swing them out from the ships side, run up the fire pumps to simulate an emergency and generally look positive and ready for action.

Board of Trade Sports

On one trip we had a new second engineer full of energy and bright ideas. He decided to test the crew's effectiveness by ringing the alarm bells on a Thursday, bad mistake!

The crew ignored all the usual safety measures like closing water tight doors, running out fire hoses and instead adopted the age old adage 'woman and children first'. In this case it was crew first followed by Singer sewing machines and bicycles.

The sight of the lifeboats packed with our sweaty crew clutching cardboard suitcases and sitting on top of a pile of bikes and sewing machines was not quite what the second intended. We never again ran unscheduled drills mores the pity.

Our shipping orders came through giving me the opportunity to go through the Suez Canal. Fighting off the aforementioned 'gilly gilly' men I watched the banks slipping by, green on one side desert on the other with remnants of tanks lying abandoned in the sand.

Ships went through in a convoy at a slow speed stopping in the middle to let the oncoming ships by. Along the banks Arab life went on, washing their clothes in the green water, fishing and going about their ablutions at a leisurely pace undisturbed by the passage of ships slipping by.

Down below in the control room I was on the throttle keeping the engine revs just ticking over at slow ahead with the standby crew checking the hundreds of dials and gauges sipping sweet tea and gossiping as old sea dogs do. Suddenly the control room door burst open and in an alcoholic haze the chief staggered in clutching a wheel spanner and promptly pushed me off the throttle. Obviously on a promise in Port Said he pushed the revs up and glared at the assembled somewhat confused engineers. Not half as surprised as the Captain and the mates on the bridge who suddenly found the ship getting far too close to the ship in front! Like a stack of dominoes one by one the complete convoy were forced to speed up until the whole fleet was roaring along the canal.

Now the Suez Canal is fairly narrow and the combined bow waves of several thousand tons of ships had an interesting effect on the level of water. The previously gently rippling water turned into a tidal wave sweeping along the banks and flooding over into the fields. The laundrymen, fishermen and scrubbers all rapidly became swimmers as they tried desperately to avoid getting sucked under the ships and minced by the whirling props. Not easy wearing Speedo bed sheets or whatever the Arabs national dress is called. If someone had a stopwatch I'm convinced the one hundred metre freestyle record was smashed. It brings a whole new meaning to riding along on the crest of a wave!

The chief was eventually brought to his senses or more aptly lost his senses with a well timed blow to the head and was shipped back home from Port Said

The same Chief Engineer had an irritating night time habit. He would drink all evening then stagger down below and fall about the control room adjusting things that didn't need adjusting. Consequently when he had lurched off back to the bar, an alarm would sound in the duty engineer's cabin causing him to rush below to remedy the drunken chiefs fumbling.

A game plan was devised to halt the chief's nocturnal control room visits. We stuffed an old boiler suit full of straw, lashed some engine room boots on its feet and making a head of rags taped a yellow helmet on top. We sat the effigy in the watch keepers chair and made it slump over the control desk with a can of Castle lager held in its gloved hand.

Turning the control room lights down low we all hid in the clean workshop, which boasted a large viewing window. The dummy looked eerily realistic bathed a red hue from the alarm panel.

On cue the chief staggered in and proceeded to give our straw friend the bollocking of its lifetime. The highlight of the piece was when the chief took a swipe at the slumbering dummy making the helmeted head fly off and roll around the floor. With a cry like a wounded banshee the chief took off up the engine room steps straight to the bar where we found him talking to a huge glass of whisky.

The night time visits stopped from then on.

Eventually we sailed back into the UK, back to real life 'but not as we know it Jim' to quote Star Trek. Somehow life in good old 'blighty' had lost its sparkle.

First born Jeremy had swallowed the anchor and took the 'Ten Pound Pom' ticket to Australia. Think of Australia as the island of endless beaches, blue seas, sun and the odd kangaroo. It also has several deadly insects, spiders, snakes, scorpions, sharks and crocs. Billy Connolly has been known to say 'how the fuck does any Aussie make it through to adulthood with all the monsters that live in that far off land'. I still fancied giving it a go.

(I'm actually supping an ice cold beer five miles from the Sydney opera house editing this missive but let's not confuse the issue, that's for another book)

Tying the Knot

Sally, have I mentioned her? Anyway she and I decided to get married, have one final trip to sea then emigrate to Sydney. One more trip to Shropshire to ask her father for her daughters hand and a date was set. February bound to be freezing but what the heck I was in love. Invitations were sent out, Sally had tons of relatives, I just had me 'bruvs', so I invited some ex girlfriends to make up the numbers. Sally's spinster aunts lived in a great mansion in the backwoods of Shropshire, inhabiting just the west wing of their building. They had acres of land including a farm cottage for the newlyweds to fornicate in as bride and groom do!

As ever the most important part of a wedding is the stag night so the lads laid on a splendid evening. Meeting in London we drank a few pubs dry as they tried to see me under the table. One by one I out drunk them until a particular lethal cocktail took my legs away. Sensing victory Ox dragged the survivors around Soho. Dressed in a pair of crutchless panties I viewed a seedy strip show from the floor until a very large bouncer ejected us into the street. A mini bus whisked us away to safety back to Steve's parent's house the scene of many a Xmas party. To round the evening off the lads lashed me to lamppost on the Great North road and went to bed. Releasing myself I broke into the house exposed myself to Dotty and Fred then fell into a drunken stupor.

So I was to be wed, Sally was a great girl a tad on the strange side but hey am I normal? Answers on a postcard please!

Ox took me for a quiet drink and asked for the final time, 'am you sure', 'yes I said' with fingers tightly crossed behind me, and so it was to be.

We drove up to Shropshire to the aunts house where a do it yourself reception was being prepared with all my pals turning too, laying tables and later their girlfriends in the makeshift dormitories. Sally had a fit of the nerves, decided she didn't love me and panicked. The ceremony went ahead, a candlelit service, all very romantic except the bloody candles blew out every time someone entered the church and my brown velvet suit caught fire as I stood too close to a particularly large flame.

The congregation was a mixed bunch, all of Sally's relations on one side, a fierce looking mob as I recall, spinster Aunts with moustaches in the main. On my side Mum and Dad had excelled themselves. Father looked like Monty and mother was wearing an Indian peg seller's outfit brought back from father's recent visit to the sub continent!

The 1st marriage Buster, Mum, Joff, me, Sally, Pop and Dee.
(note fire proof velvet suit)

All my pals were there anticipating the bit when the

priest asked the congregation whether there was anyone here who knows any reason that we should not get married etc etc and as the rest of my guests were my old girlfriends I dare say there were.

It was a great party in fact as Ox was later to say 'fantastic piss up pity you had to spoil it by getting married'!

We danced and drank until two then drove off across the field to our tiny unheated farm cottage to find Ox had put six pounds of wet liver in the marital bed. Sally not being aware that he was reminding me of my evening with Jill the Pill in Durban thought how thoughtful of him to provide breakfast but why wasn't it in the fridge.

The very kind Aunts had visited the cottage earlier to make an apple pie bed or whatever they called that quaint custom and had left disgusted taking with them Ox's obscene note which had been stuck to the offal.

The stopcock for the loo was shut and was sited somewhere in the yard. So to allow my new bride the pleasure of dispensing of some of the many gallons of hooch we had consumed I spent a merry hour up to my neck in mud and other less salubrious farm debris searching for the damn thing. By the time I got back mission accomplished expecting my conjugal rights Sally was sitting in the car clutching an armful of old horse blankets panicking that our guests would be cold in their dormitories.

Back to the great house we drove, with a shrinking ardour and to be truthful well pissed off to find the party still in full swing. 'I had better stay here and make sure all is OK', I ventured, so slightly 'sniffly' she returned to the cottage.

When I woke up I was in a heap next to Ox who announced it had dumped three feet of snow in the night so we went tobogganing, well why not, doesn't every newlywed take to the slopes on their first morning.

As the guests made their departure I felt a shiver down my back, no more the gay bachelor, shit what have I done?

Wendy, an old flame, and her flashy boyfriend's departure restored my good spirits. As they drove away in his sports car he waved and raised his electric window, which unfortunately pinned his toupee to the roof and stuck there as he gunned the engine. The sight of old baldy with his rug hanging behind him kept me smiling until my first pint.

I had applied to Australia house for Sally and I to emigrate, an easy task in those days as dear brother Jeremy lived in Sydney. Subject to an interview we were in. As the lift door closed in Australia house the old lift attendant asked, 'where to', 'Sydney' I answered brightly. The controlled look that crossed his countenance gave me a clue that he might have heard that line a few times before. So we were in but first the stuff of dreams Sally was coming with me on my last trip on an old Clan boat as an officer's wife to India.

It was a sort of second honeymoon as the first had been a trifle spoilt by Sally's insistence that her sister came along as a chaperone. On reflection I wouldn't have minded if her sister had come as my conjugal rights were still to be satisfied!

We joined the Clan Macgregor in Glasgow and set sail to India at the fine old speed of seven knots, poor old girl she was a little bit knackered and the ship was tired as well.

Life was paradise, we had our own Indian steward who was at Sally's beck and call and months of hot sunny days exploring the coast of India ahead of us but little did I know the storm clouds were once again gathering. Twelve officers, Sally, the captain's wife and fifty odd Indian crewmen, inhabited our little ship ploughing its slow passage across the oceans.

Ten days out the air conditioning irreparably broke down, the 'punkha louvres' just emitting a whisper of hot humid air. Cardboard air deflectors sprouted along the ships side trying to force some air into the stifling cabins, without much success. Sally slept fitfully on our cabin bed whilst I slept on the floor with my head by the door catching the slight breeze that ran down the alleyway.

It was in this strange position that I caught a glimpse of a face at the porthole staring at my wives naked body which I quite naturally took offence to so seizing the nearest object that came to hand, sandalwood Indian elephant, I hurled it at the intruder. A muffled oath followed by running footsteps indicated my aim had been true.

The next morning at breakfast I was surprised to find Andy the third mate absent, normally he would be eating away before our eight to twelve morning watch. The reason became clear at lunchtime when he appeared with a small elephant shaped bruise on his right cheek.

There is an unwritten rule of the sea, which states that officer's wives on board are out of bounds i.e. not to be pursued and wooed by other officers. I had actively encouraged Sally to visit the bridge to learn about navigating to give her something to do, surely nothing was going on, it was our honeymoon after all.

I challenged the third mate as to why he was looking through my porthole which he first denied but had to admit he had glanced through on his way to bed, the elephant bruise would have been hard to explain away!

I talked with Sally but she just laughed it off, 'you're being paranoid' she said, maybe I was but there was an uncomfortable atmosphere in our cabin and it wasn't the curry.

BBQ's on deck, old films showed by the cadets and the burning sun smoothed away my worries, soon we would be in India, time to go up the road together exploring the bazaars and markets of this fascinating country.

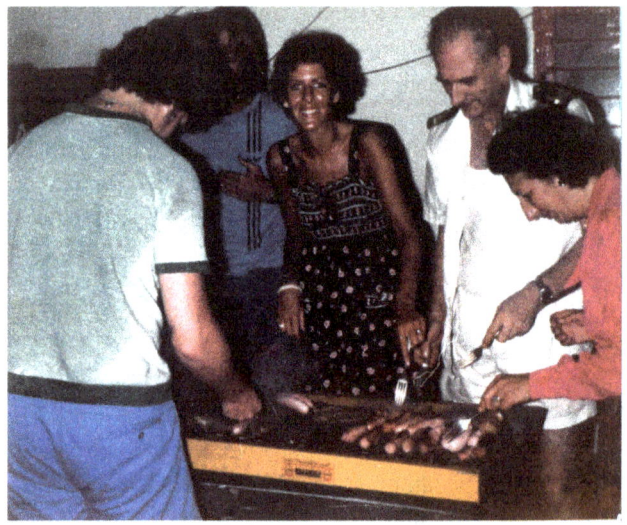
Sally. BBQ on deck and its very hot

One Sunday the storm clouds broke, I could hear drunken shouting from the officer's mess as I made my way for pre lunch drinks. Opening the mess door I found a very pissed highly belligerent third mate informing the assembled officers how much he loved my wife, how much she reciprocated the feeling and how they were going to live together after the trip and fuck what her husband felt.

Even after all these years as I write this, rolling my guts out in an Atlantic storm I still can recall the sense of anger, shame and hopelessness. I had enjoyed the company of so many women and had married a girl who was unfaithful on our honeymoon, what a fucking world! Sensing me at the door Andy, throwing punches madly bundled me into the corridor. Rolling around ducking the blows I could see the drink had taken effect on his timing as he missed every time. All bar one when a wild haymaker whistled over my head and neatly chinned the captain's wife who had left the saloon to find out what the commotion was. Sally was banned off deck, I was charged to keep control of her and the third mate was cautioned.

The next week as we toiled our way through the Indian Ocean was agony until Bombay finally appeared on the horizon. Bundling Sally and all her possessions into a taxi I sent her flying home, off the ship and out of my life but as it transpired not for long.

I was desolated, I felt anger, jealousy, hate but more a sense of what the hell went wrong, for once in my life I had made a commitment and it had got up and smacked me in the face.

The next few weeks tramping around India's ports were a misery, I longed for the trip to be over so I didn't have to see the smirk on the third mates face every day. Even the delights of Bombay the hustle and bustle, the old English taxis driven at breakneck speed by curry crazed Abduls couldn't relieve the hurt burning inside me, yes it still wasn't the curries.

We finally loaded our last cargo and waddled our way around Africa through Biscay and finally into Birkenhead. I had phoned Ox from the English Channel asking him to come and get me from this hell ship. He was naturally agog with curiosity, Sally had reappeared saying there was a problem on the ship and filled in no further details.

As he walked up the gangplank I felt this huge release of emotion at last a true friend to unburden all the hurt. Behind him with barefaced cheek was Sally, she had persuaded Ox to bring her so she could see her husband but disappeared immediately in the general direction of the third mate's cabin, well I never.

Greeting my pal warmly I excused myself and sped off after her. I omitted to tell you the third mate was built like a brick shithouse but honour was at stake so I let fly with all the pain and misery I could muster. It was a bit one sided but I got a few in before I smacked him in the fist with my chin and kicked him in the foot with my bollocks. Ox astounded grabbed the back of my shirt, which promptly disintegrated, as did I. 'Get me off this fucking ship' I cried as I packed up my bags, my sea life and my marriage and walked for the last time off the ship little realising by this act I had 'swallowed the anchor'.

Swallowing the anchor

Leaving the sea has been known for ever as swallowing the anchor, a bit perverse as I am currently in the middle of the Atlantic again, on Wizzo taking part in my fourth ARC. Don't books take a long time to write?

The atmosphere was a little chilly in the car as we drove away from the docks and became positively glacial as I argued with Sally until dropping her off somewhere. At last I could tell Ox and Tessa his wife or wife to be all the problems of the last few months. A problem shared is a problem halved or some such similar nonsense but talking my tale of woe through helped me enormously. I stayed the night with Ox and his family where we poured copious amounts of alcohol down our necks and for the first time in months I slept.

The demons came for me at five am, what am I going to do, what have I got left in the world, why did she leave me, all mixed up with a very unhealthy hangover!

Somewhat surprisingly my parent's attitude was less than sympathetic, 'you must have done something to upset her they said' so I took myself off to the pub for a rethink of life. I saw an advert for a cheap holiday in Benidorm of all places so booked it and flew the next day. Benidorm out of season is okay. I met a gang of girls so had a week on the bevy and I think some personal attention from one of them, surprising how a sob story can be such a good chat up line.

Sitting back in the grey prison I pondered my fate, feeling bloody miserable I went to the doctor for help. He prescribed some drugs to make me sleep and probably forget about everything. I looked at the prescription and thought, so what your marriage has failed, you've got no job or place to live but for Gods sake at least I've travelled and seen some things!

The prescription went into the trashcan and I went off to find work.

Speed to meet your Need

I saw an ad in the Telegraph for Nu Swift fire extinguishers. It read, interesting work, get to meet people and sell top of the range fire extinguishers. I had attended many fire fighting courses at sea as well as experiencing the real thing, you remember our charlady's two attempts at arson, so I jumped a train to London.

The interviews were to be held in a very large and old London hotel whose foyer was full of a rare mix of humanity all supposed experts on fire fighting. After registering I watched the mob as they were called up to the interview room and watched as they returned all looking happy, did they all pass the test?

Finally my name was called so I knocked on the door and strode in. The room was large with a desk and two chairs in front of a big window with red velvet curtains. A smallish chap with a slightly shiny suit shook my hand and started the usual questions.

I thought my qualifications matched their needs and agreed that no I had never sold anything before but I was outgoing and as it was commission only what was their problem. Suddenly in mid sentence the guy pulled out a can of fuel poured it on the table and set fire to it, shouting 'now what are you going to do'. Thinking the guy had gone mad I jumped up, ripped the red velvet curtain down, and smothered the fire.

'Fuck me' he said 'no one's ever done that before, you're supposed to panic and I put out the fire with this', in his hand was a great bit of kit a Nu Swift fire extinguisher. 'Well you've got the job congratulations, be at the Grimsdyke hotel up north somewhere for your weeks training then you're on your way'. Stumbling out of the hotel I thought what sort of company is this that frightens people into buying their wares by setting fire to their property, still beggars can't be choosers.

I bought a little white mini and buzzed up the motorway and booked myself into the hotel. I was sharing a room with one of the guys I'd seen at the interviews. He had an enormous bag, which filled the room and made interesting chinking and clanking noises when delved into. 'Care for a drink' he politely asked so thinking churlish not to we had a very convivial night. He reminded me of the chap David Niven shared some time with in the 'Moons a Balloon', read it it's a great book.

Next day slightly blurred we sat in a meeting room and had the week's syllabus explained. Basically there was a big book all about fires and fire extinguishers and we had to learn it, oh and some practical stuff. At the end of the week we would sit an exam and if we passed we would be assigned an area and Nu Swift people we would be, fine.

I met a chamber maid after a couple of nights in the hotel. After sampling some very stiff drinks from my mates bag she led me into a spare room for some help with my book learning, call it what you like. On the final night we had a bit of a party despite being told to have a sober quiet night before the exam!

My friendly maid was helping me with the buzz sayings, such as speed to meet your need, as she tugged at me energetically and do you know how fast the spray leaves the nozzle? As fast as an express train and I'm pleased to say she demonstrated both nozzle and spray.

Stumbling sleepily back along the corridor in dawn's faint light I bumped into the examiner on her way for an early breakfast, I suppose it would have helped if I had my trousers on. She sniffed her disapproval and made some comment about 'fact chance you've got Buster' and bustled past me.

Well the exam was a joke, a pet chimpanzee would

have passed, in fact I'm not sure if one didn't!

At the prize giving ceremony we were all awarded certificates, a briefcase containing the manual, a petrol tray and a full brand new all singing Nu Swift fire extinguisher. As an added bonus we all got a car sticker with speed to meet your need emblazoned on it much to the joy of my chambermaid who insisted on one more demonstration and to the disgust of one of my new work mates who only had a push bike.

'Stick it on your cross bar' said a kindly new boss, 'stick it up your arse' he replied rhetorically!

Fixing my sticker proudly in the back of the mini I sped southwards to fame and fortune, or so I thought.

My parents lived in the back of beyond where the only fires were lit by farmers to burn off the crops, somehow I thought even a Nu Swift couldn't cope with their conflagrations.

Once more I had thrown myself on the mercies of the Oxley family which was handy as my patch as us salesmen called it was Chigwell and Woodford just a spit from Brentwood in my company vehicle the battered mini.

On my first morning resplendent in my only suit I set off with my packed lunch made for me by the ever patient Dick Oxley, you remember he was the one who said I exam results weren't everything on the sailing club wall, I wonder what he thought now?

I pulled into a row of shops and studied my handbook. Introduce yourself and the company and ask have you a fire extinguisher. There are only two answers, yes I have, or no I haven't, piece of piss. If they haven't then point out that according to the factory act they have to have an extinguisher for so many square feet of office or factory space. If they have an extinguisher and it's a competitor's product then examine it preferably tutting, condemn it then sell them one of your own.

Seemed easy enough, so grasping my shiny new briefcase I strolled into a sweetshop and waited in line behind a crowd of school kids busy nicking sweets and ordering fags. Eventually I faced the proprietor, a Mr Singh who uttered these immortal words, 'are you a salesman', 'yes' I replied, well I was trying to be one, 'then bugger off', so off I buggered to study the manual for more hints in selling.

Some customers will be short with you it said and they didn't come much shorter than Mr Singh. This was a new experience for me, all my life I had walked into shops and businesses and had been treated with courtesy, well not in Barclay's banks obviously. Straightening my shoulders I walked into the next shop a butchers. Not letting this guy get in first and remembering our friendly red faced big handed family butcher I said 'Robin Tickner, Nu Swift, have you any extinguishers', there it was done.

'Yes I have actually but it may be out of date' he said 'would you like to look at it'?

So I shook it and 'tutted' as the good book described and sighed, that was my own invention, 'I think this needs replacing and by the factory act you will need several more'. This troubled the man, 'how much'? Well in truth we were expensive but as I was only on commission we needed to be, gasping at the price he offered objections.

As a highly trained and experienced sales man, it was my second call after all, I knew how to overcome any reticence, 'it's not that much are you Jewish or something'. 'Yes I am' and wheeled me outside to look at his sign, Cohen's Kosher Butchers and slammed the door in my face! So lesson learned always look at the sign above the door before entering!

The faithful manual offered this advice, if meeting

with resistance try another area and type of business, so I drove off and spied an old haberdashery. Wool, cottons all you need for your home boasted the shop sign complete with faded knitting patterns from knitting monthly in the shop window. Something stirred in my mind, turning the page to wool shops I found this chilling information.

Danger of spontaneous combustion. Some materials like wool and straw when packed down have some form of chemical reaction that can cause a fire. This was more like it; I'll scare the arse of the proprietor and get a sale. Opening the door to a gentle tinkle I found a pleasant looking lady in a twin set idling through a Woman's Realm.

After introducing myself she said 'so glad to see you, one of your engineers was in last week and said my extinguisher needed replacing would you like to check it' So following the aforementioned procedure I clinched my first sale, yippee twenty smackers in my pocket.

After filling out the copious paperwork I remembered the book, when you have sold one try for another. Looking out the back window I saw an old cardboard caravan. 'You like caravanning I asked' 'oh yes my husband and me often take the baby away at weekends'. Sensing a kill I asked 'whether they had a Nu swift in the van as what with the calor gas cooker and cardboard construction they were in danger of it bursting into flames at any time'.

A troubled look came over her, 'let me demonstrate' I offered and we went out to the back yard. Giving the baby's pram a gentle rock to show her I liked children although I couldn't eat a whole one I set up my pitch. The caravan door was open with a curtain gently fluttering in the slight breeze as I poured petrol into the tray and set it alight and most impressive it looked.

'What are you doing' she gasped, 'fear not, just watch this' I said as I pulled out my Nu Swift.

Speed to meet your need, the spray will come out as fast as an express train, unfortunately it was a British rail train as nothing happened. In my keenness I had demonstrated it to all my mates hoping for easy sales so the bloody thing was empty. Resorting to desperate measures I kicked the tray causing the flames to roar up and catch the curtain on fire.

The baby began to cough from the fumes as I stamped the flames out, pulled the curtain off the door and grabbing my bits thanked the lady for her order. Excusing myself I exited to the sound of her threatening to call the police. Still a sale is a sale.

Over the next few weeks I demonstrated to lady hairdressers, video shops, post offices in fact anyone who would listen, with mixed results. In the end I worked mornings and went to kids matinees at the cinema in the afternoons, well it was cheap entertainment and it was the school holidays. I saw Jungle Book ten times, I was word perfect on 'I'm the king of the swingers' and I can still do a passable impression of Sheer Khan the tiger.

Head office rang me one day concerned over my sales or lack of sales and arranged for me to go out with the regional manager the following week. He was a veteran of Nu Swift a nice man who turned out to be a fantastic salesman. Every call we took an order, I didn't twig it was fixed until he sold one to an East London undertaker.

I was watching the carpenters planing and sanding the coffins all cheerfully whistling to Terry Wogan coming out of a coffin shaped radio, the brass handles being the tuner and volume controls when the truth hit me. Corpses don't spontaneous combust, sure they catch fire but only in crematoriums, as in Little Johnny, 'sorry I wasn't at school yesterday my granddad got burnt'. Miss, 'sorry to hear that, not badly I hope'. Little Johnny, 'well they don't fuck about in the crematorium Miss'.

At lunch I challenged the manager who agreed the sales were all rigged but it usually gave new salesman confidence. He did however have a fund of good experiences, this is my favourite.

One day he walked into a big factory to meet the site engineer. Going through the factory act bit the engineer admitted there wasn't a fire appliance in the place and called the chairman down to discuss the implications. As they dithered our man offered to demonstrate his appliance.

A good place to have a controllable fire is in a toilet so off they went to the workman's latrines. Pouring petrol into the pan, incanting speed to meet your need there was a woof of flames instantly extinguished to the admiring nods of the assembled throng. Back they went to the boardroom to work out what was to be a very profitable order.

The postscript is not quite so satisfactory especially for old Ted the night watchman. As usual after finishing his rounds Ted with his copy of the Sun tucked under his arms would go for his morning ablutions. As luck would have it the only cubicle available was the scene of the recent demonstration. Settling himself comfortably down he lit his fag, took an appreciative drag and dropped the still burning match into the pan.

At the hospital after sewing half his arse back on they told him how lucky he was. 'How the fuck do you work that one out, having a quiet shit and the management nearly blow my dick off'?

The next weekend I went to visit my parents via a couple of drinking houses and suitably anaesthetised I stumbled in to find a dinner party in full swing. A new and captive audience I thought and swung into my sales pitch. When I had finished one of the guests, Ron Trig a RAF type with clipped moustache and pipe in mouth puffed reflectively and said, 'I've got a fire extinguisher but how about coming to work for me'.

He was a product manager for Bosch power tools, 'we have a new construction line coming out' he said 'and we need someone with engineering skills and the balls to sell it'. Well I had both in abundance, skills not balls you understand, the only snag being the job didn't start until January and it was only September. A long winter of discontent loomed.

I spent one more week demonstrating those bloody fire extinguishers to bemused hairdressers, video shops, and sweet shops in fact anyone who would let me through their doors.

My mate Ox as ever came up with a solution. He was an up and coming star with the largest house builder in Essex with sites all over the county. One particular site had a huge theft problem. Between Friday night and Monday morning half the stores would disappear from the supposedly secure compound. He offered me a job as labourer come spy to watch out for the criminals and turn them in and as a plus I would get good site experience for my new job. Too good an offer to refuse I stupidly thought.

Monday morning with yet more Dick Oxley sandwiches in my mini, wearing those provocative builders bum jeans I reported to the site manager.

Within a week I was a builder, I could wolf whistle at the girls and shout obscene suggestions. Nail banging and hitting thumbs with lurid language was a speciality as was page three of the Sun reading and most importantly I knew how to sweep all the rubbish under baths and screw the panel in afterwards. If ever

Michael Fish denies another hurricane and you live in one of the houses that I built don't worry you have a half a ton of hardcore under your bath to hold your house down.

So as not to blow my cover Ox and I agreed not to talk on site. One wet and rainy day with the site a muddy quagmire he roared up in his brand new shiny black Alfa Romeo as I turned onto the road covered in mud driving a dumper. Choosing a particularly deep puddle I gunned my engine and sprayed his car, 'new company dumper' I shouted as I disappeared in a swirl of diesel smoke. My reputation as a bit of a site maverick was thus enhanced so aiding my spying operation.

Spying was easy, just walk around to the compound on a Friday night to see the guys backing up to the gate which had been scaled by one of the nimble lads, pick the padlock then place your order. Taps, copper pipes, sinks, boilers, doors whole houses for all I knew were chucked over the fence into the vans and away.

I decided to go undercover and joined the queue, it's surprising how much kit you can get in the back of a mini, I became that bloke down the pub who can get you anything, know what I mean!

The Indian summer passed and the cold grey prison spread its icy tentacles around me, freezing dark mornings wading through icy puddles, spade over shoulder, how or why the fuck do we live here. Sure builders, 'chippies', plasterers, plumbers and me the labourer have great summers, dark tans and a weekly brown envelope stuffed with drink vouchers but sod the winter.

I have nothing but admiration for our construction guys for what they have to put up with, I suppose you could include farmers, cops traffic wardens, no strike the last bastards out, I wish.

I was dumped recently on my fiftieth birthday by some city filly who viewed my prospects, a boat in the Caribbean and a tiny room in Burnham as financially non viable and ran off with a rich motor boat owner.

Before realising the imbalance between her expectations and my bank balance she had blagged two free holidays on my yacht. What's that got to do with traffic wardens I hear you say, well broken hearted I staggered back from our tearful finale to find my car had been clamped. What else can go wrong, it's the final straw, thank you so much God I thought shaking my fist at the heavens John Cleese style as I bawled my heart out. Still at least the callous bitch had the decency to pay the fine there and then as we parted on a cold and rainy London street. Money doesn't mend a broken heart though. Now I don't want you to feel sorry for me, I have been a right bastard myself in the past and I deeply regret some of the stupid things I have done with woman.

Sitting here once again in the middle of the ocean some two hundred miles from Bermuda you get time to think things out, if the typing is a bit blurred it's maybe due to a few tears of remorse.

Oh bugger it back to the plot but I promise I'll come back to the London girl maybe to offer some advice so perhaps you won't get suckered by nice tits and a pretty face. It's what's inside that counts the honesty, faithfulness, love and support that we all need to be happy.

(And you thought I was a shallow bastard.)

The Bosch Years

January at last, suffering from the usual New Year hangover after partying with the gang in Padstow in Cornwall, I received a letter from Ron Trigg inviting me to Bosch head office in Watford for a formal interview.

Donning the suit I took my faithful mini to Rhodes Way Watford and stood outside the huge shiny building. Taking a deep breath I strode in to find Ron standing there hand outstretched, 'welcome to Bosch power tools' he said shaking my hand warmly.

My interview well I think that's what it was took place in the Red Lion pub in Radlet over several pints, the upshot being I was the new construction rep covering all of the UK and I started next Monday. 'What exactly will I be doing' I asked, with a puff of pipe smoke Ron replied, 'selling concrete vibratory machines to bridge, tunnel and large construction sites'. Well whatever he was talking about I was up for it especially as my business card had Robin Tickner Vibrator Specialist printed on it, should cause a stir with the ladies I thought.

My itinerary included four weeks of training at head office then one week out with Tony Payne one of the old hands to show me the ropes. I soon found out that the product training was easy it was getting to know how to deal with the bureaucracy of a large company and a German one to boot that was the difficult bit.

Ron lived in Worthing or Costa Geriatric, as it was better known so he lived all week in the Spiders Web motel in Watford known and loved by all sales representatives. This was to be my home for the next month or should have been until fate played its hand. This is a typical booking in procedure at the Spiders Web.

Receptionist, 'how can I help you sir'

Rep, 'I'd like a room for the week please'.

Receptionist,' would that be a single or a double'.

Experienced Rep, 'a double at single corporate rate please, and I would like one with ripped sheets, peeling ceiling, non functioning shower and toilet and near the M1 so the traffic noise will keep me awake all night please'.

Receptionist, 'certainly sir all our rooms are like that'.

So why did we all stay there, well it was near the office, adjacent to several good pubs and it had a grab a granny night every Wednesday. Let me explain, a well meaning organisation ran weekly meetings named Divorced, Single or Separated, DSS for short, in the hotels ballroom where like minded people could meet to discuss their problems and socialise.

They should have called it Divorced, Single, Separated and drunken horny sales reps club. Once you had offered false credentials to the crone on the door and received your yellow membership card you went upstairs. The dance floor and bar were deliberately dimly lit where people stumbled around bumping into the furniture trying to find someone vaguely attractive, it was like meeting people using Braille.

The reps advantage was that we could whip our prey back to our hotel room to finish off the process. Mind you when the lights were switched up at midnight you could see what you had been talking to all night, there were many hasty retreats beaten from both sexes.

On my first Thursday night of Bosch employment Ron called an early halt to my training explaining it was social club night, which would give me a good opportunity to meet other members of the company. I was keen on the idea as during my wanderings around the vast offices I had chanced upon the typing pool, strange description, makes you think of bikini clad girls on lilos typing away on their Remington's.

The club turned out to be the canteen, which was a bit of a disappointment, but it was full of totty. One young lady Ron introduced me to turned out to be in charge of checking the reps expense sheets. 'You won't get anything pass me' she said coyly accepting one of many gin and tonics. Later in the back seat of her Morris 1100 my naked arse sore from the plastic leopard skin seat covers I thought just my luck to get caught 'flagrante' in the Bosch staff car park in my first week.

I moved in with her the next week so she could fully explain how to fiddle your expenses. In those halcyon days before computer generated receipts, all hotels, petrol stations, and restaurants in fact anywhere us gentlemen of the road made claimable purchases, receipts were hand written.

A typical hotel proprietor would ask how much do you want to appear on your bill, similarly favourite eating houses and even the local garage would often join in the scam. For a couple of years whenever I visited the office I would stay with leopard skin, take her out for dinner and get a phoney receipt from a friendly hotel. Actually it cost the company less, I got to stay in a house instead of a bloody hotel and got my leg over, seemed fair to me.

Eventually I was allowed out travelling with Tony who covered North Wales, I remember the kind welcome we received from the dealers not only because Tony had been calling on them for many years but we represented Bosch which had a reputation for quality. Such is the value of branding.

We stayed in commercial travellers accommodation as reps were grandly known. As well as a bar and dining saloon the hotel boasted a reps room where we sat at tall desks writing out our orders taken during the day. This was long before fax and mobile phones, the internet had not even been dreamed of.

Bosch had several divisions the largest being automotive, if you look under the bonnet of your car you would be amazed to see how many of the components are Bosch. ABS systems, electronic ignition, spark plugs windscreen wipers and supplying the music a Blaupunkt car radio.

Bosch cookers, microwaves, fridge's are on the wish lists of most ladies of the house and Bosch Power tools eventually became brand leader in the UK with a lot of help from myself he pompously added!

Pratt with a moustache

Roger Varney was my regional manager and confidant and despite ups and downs we still correspond some twenty-five years later.

Roger explained the reporting procedure. Every week a proposed itinerary had to be supplied reaching him by the preceding Friday with a weekly report showing how successful I had been, and the infamous two weekly expenses sheet. A monthly report covering market forces, competitor activity and pricing was also required.

Some weeks you felt you couldn't go out to visit customers as you had too much paperwork to do. On top of all these reports were six weekly call plans to fabricate plus an ABC customer analysis, oh how reps love paperwork!

I called on all the big construction companies, the Dartford Tunnel contractors, hire companies, now there's a rough and ready breed, in fact anyone who poured concrete. I was selling huge vibrators just like the ones our ladies use but bigger powered by three phase motors. These were plunged into poured cement to create a much stronger mix. The fact they were five times the cost of British ones may have something to do with my lack of sales.

On the social side I was sail boat racing every weekend out in the North Sea competing in the East Anglian Offshore Racing Association otherwise known as getting freezing cold visiting pearls of the East coast. West Mersea, Lowestoft, Harwich, Ramsgate and for a special treat Ostende. Wow. I was sharing a flat with another Robin who was an epileptic, he only had one turn and that was the night he met me, funny the effect I have on people!

A hippy couple lived next door who were quite fond of exotic substances. Unfortunately their habit progressed to heavier drugs with tragic consequences. One night I was awoken by frantic banging on our front door. Opening it I found the bloke completely stoned. 'Mary is gone man' he slurred and staggered back into his flat. 'Where is she' I said but he just slumped to the ground. The hall was dimly lit with one of those lights with bubbles of oil glooping about so I pushed the dining room door open against some resistance.

Stepping into the dark room the door slammed shut behind me closed by the arm of the stone dead young girl who had collapsed in the corner. I was too angry to be frightened she was only fifteen; it made me stay away from the drug scene for many years. The ambulance guys who took her away had several choice words to say to the still stoned boy friend, I thought a good slap might have been applicable too.

Richards's sister Judy, who had turned from a gawky fourteen-year old into a real stunner, had many equally stunning friends who she foolishly introduced me to.

Glynne was beautiful with a perfect complexion which only took an hour to apply! I spent most of the time during our short relationship waiting for the paint to dry. For her birthday I bought her a can of Nitramors. I had a rival for her affections who happened to find her car outside my flat one evening so he vandalised mine. John and I still smile about that now. My car and listen to this was a Mark 3 Cortina estate, British racing green with beefed up yellow rear shock absorbers, impressive eh!

Godzilla was another of Judy's friends, now they were breasts you could die for and probably would do if you fell into them. After a few more friends had succumbed to my charms Judy said that if she was going to be my pimp she wanted paying.

The other Robin had promotion and was moving on so I needed a new place to live.

The Navigators Story

Jones the Navigator

One of my brother Jeremy's pals from schooldays Alan, had sadly lost his wife. Rattling about in his now empty house he made me an offer to be his lodger, which I readily accepted. Alan is one of the nicest guys around and in later years I was proud to be his stand in best man due to Jeremy residing in Australia. Alan and I shared many a pint in the pubs of Brentwood and Shenfield deep in the heart of Essex commuter land.

Mildly eccentric he papered his downstairs loo with nautical charts so he could plan future voyages whilst enthroned. He also had a miracle cure for the common cold which he named the night nurse slammer. Ingredients, liquid night nurse, the green stuff which carried a warning not to drive agricultural machinery, why would you? And a bottle of scotch, it worked every time. Some time later, usually about two days, you woke up without a cold but with a dreadful hangover, such is life.

I introduced Alan to Richard Oxley and he became one of the crew on Richards's latest offshore racing boat. He quickly fast tracked to the position of navigator bypassing me and the other lads sitting with our legs over the side as we crashed through the cold wet North Sea. Racing across the channel one dark night we had completed several circuits of the racing buoys off Harwich and frankly we were lost. The role of navigator cut a fine line between sitting nice and warm down below working out positions and carrying the can when we ended up on a sand bank. Navigation aids were fairly rudimental this was long before satellite navigation. We used a RDF (radio direction finder) it was really a radio with a compass stuck on top and wildly inaccurate especially on a tiny storm tossed sail boat. Trying to pick up signals from ships buoys which all had individual signals to home in on we all reckoned Jones was listening to the cricket scores. Any way after waving this gadget around in the general direction of land he disappeared below to do some guesswork. Frustrated Richard shouted 'where the fuck are we' to which Jones gravely announced 'in the middle of Colchester high street, outside Woolworth's to be exact'. Now that for Jones was fairly accurate!

With the advent of Decca the predecessor of satellite navigation, Alan's navigating got marginally better. On another weekend we were delivering the boat down to the South coast from Burnham on Crouch for Cowes week. It became apparent we or rather he was lost due to the mass of frantic calculations covering the chart and the undercover shaking of the ju ju beads.

'It's not easy' he cried 'there are no bloody signposts out here'. Unfortunately for Alan a few minutes later a signpost drifted by washed away by the high tide, we all gave him a long meaningful look. In his favour the sign did say public footpath which wasn't much use, at least it could have indicated to where the path went, to give him a clue.

I'm warming to my task.

On another delivery trip from Burnham to the South coast we hit a gale and had to bare pole it into Brighton marina, scary stuff. We followed one of the tall ships into the tiny entrance and watched her roll so heavily one of her yards hit the marina wall. We had been at sea for three days, soaked to the skin, tired and hungry. After securing the boat we ran to the shower block and fully clothed jumped under the showers and slowly de frosted.

How are you non sailors getting on with this. Some books by such notable sailors as Josh Slocum, Peter Goss, Ellen McArthur, or Heavy Weather Sailing, Around the World in Eighty Days, Three Men in a Boat etc might help your understanding of the black art of sailing.

We tried ringing the owner Ox for help, who well I never, was in a meeting probably in some warm dry office so no joy. We decided to press on to Cowes arriving on Friday afternoon. Cold, wet, hungry, pissed off and with a thirst on! Over the radio came the owners cheery voice 'well done boys, dinner is on me after we've had a few drinks and by the way we are sleeping in the national sailing centre bunk room and as a bonus there's two girlies booked in too'

It takes an awfully long time to get from one end of Cowes high street to the other especially if you have a beer in all its fine hostelries but eventually well fed and watered we lurched back to the bunk room. Emboldened by alcohol the normally mild mannered Jones put his finger to his lips shushed us and crept in.

Tiptoeing up to one of the top bunks he grasped the blanket and ripped it back shouting 'show us your tits' he believed Ox had been spinning a line about the two girls sharing the bunk room. I don't know who was more surprised, Jones or the girl who shot bolt upright displaying all her natural charms. Red faced, mainly due to the slap she had landed, Jones apologised profusely and we gratefully settled down to sleep, well we had been at sea for quite a long time.

Alan had one more trick to play, he could snore for England, a chain saw is mute compared with this boy. He always sportingly issued a ten minute warning before starting to snore the trick being to get to sleep before the cacophony began. After he had sawn down the New Forest the two girls got up in disgust and went out to sleep on the lawn. As they left one muttered, 'I didn't mind showing my tits but now he's taking the piss'.

We had worked out a routine to stop his noise. We would put Alan on the top bunk, tie a rope around his ankle and lead it through a system of pulleys to the occupant of the lower bunk. Every time he snored a vigorous tug would lift his leg in the air thus restricting the snore. We took it in turns to be the yanker! The fact he couldn't walk in the morning due to lack of circulation was just tough titty.

One of the more demanding races on the East Coast was a RORC (Royal Ocean Racing Club) affair, demanding in that it was two hundred miles long finishing in Scheveningham in Holland. So what's wrong with that? Well they lay on a party with unending free booze that's what's wrong and they don't let you go until it's all drunk!

The race starts early Friday morning from Harwich giving the competitors Thursday night to discuss tactics. Our tactics were to start on beer have wine with dinner then into oblivion with scotch, well it had worked several times before. Alan came down by train practising his tactics in the BR buffet, missing his station and just made it for last orders. He ordered eight large whiskies which we thought was generous then drank them all himself, bastard. It was the fortieth anniversary of the race so our boat Spirit IV was packed with sailing rock stars, well us actually, and we wanted to win. Much pressure was on Alan's navigational skills, he had all the kit, sharpened pencils a new set of ju ju beads and the useless RDF.

The race took us out into the middle of the North Sea up to the Texel light ship then down the Dutch coast to Scheveningham. We made a great start hoisting our bright red spinnaker and roared away from the rest of our class sailing out to sea away from the beautiful Felixstowe coastline, cranes and all.

For some unknown reason instead of sitting in the cockpit drinking G and T's like cruising folk, the poor crew had to sit on the weather deck, legs over the rail the whole night, something to do with keeping the boat upright. All except for Alan who was waving his machine about like a man possessed and give him his due he found the bloody lightship in the middle of the night with the wind roaring and the decks awash with spray.

We finished in the early hours of the morning just in time to sample some local ale, get some sleep in ready to hit town. The free party proved a bit too much for us so we staggered back to the boat, pockets stuffed with free cigars, off to the land of nod before the passage back to Burnham. And yes we won our class!

Before we leave Alan I should mention he has a habit of falling asleep mid sentence, you carry on chatting he nods, says yeah yeah a lot and all this whilst still standing. One race week in fact the first East Anglian race week we were in the yacht club at Lowestoft. The Royal Norfolk and Suffolk don't you know old boy! Our customised support vehicle, actually an old van with a red shamrock hand painted on the side and several beds bolted in the back driven by our ever faithful mate Big Dave was our accommodation. Alan was sleep talking to the commodore. A fight broke out between some of the unruly members of our club and some locals. Being brave souls we rushed outside onto the club lawn so we could get a better view of the proceedings through the big picture windows which stood a good chance of being broken the way that the chairs were flying.

A quick headcount showed that one of our crew was missing, 'there he is' someone shouted. Fast asleep on a leather settee was Alan snoring peacefully as the battle raged around him.

After the melee died down and more restorative alcohol was downed we repaired to the van which was more comfortable and dryer than Red Shamrock our race boat lying rocking at her lines in the marina.

At three in the morning a competitor's crew decided to play a prank. Led by their skipper John Lewis the publican of the 'White Harte' pub our favoured drinking hole in Burnham they dropped a huge iron cannon on our vans back step which they had just nicked from the foyer of the yacht club. Now Big Dave does not take kindly to early morning alarms so with a roar he ran down the van to catch the perpetrators' unfortunately as his name suggests our mate carries a pound or two. The combined weight of Dave and cannon as interpreted by Newton caused the front of the van to fly into the night sky spilling us out of the rear door. John Lewis could have by rights imitated Michael Caine's infamous comment in the 'Italian Job' 'you were only supposed to blow the bloody doors off'

Several years later we got our own back on Lewis at his wedding. All his locals were dressed to the nines packed into the local church fretting through the service champing at the bit to get stuck into the reception especially the hooch. Now I'm not saying John is tight but he had reputation for deep pockets and short arms so the opportunity to drink his and new wife Linda's health was much anticipated. At the crucial moment most bachelors dread the vicar intoned 'do you Gilbert John Lewis take' the rest of the sentence was drowned out by the sailor's audible gasp of Gilbert. Oh how we enjoyed toasting Gilbert and Linda with his champagne.

Lowestoft was the scene of more nautical mayhem some years later.

EAORA ran a race from Harwich to Lowestoft on Saturday then back again on the Sunday. The race up coast used to be called the Sunk race, not because boats sunk, it was a lightship you had to round. It was a night sail until some poor 'namby pamby' yachty complained it was too dangerous and it became a day race.

We were sailing on a stripped out racer named 'Local Hero' a Briand designed thirty foot half tonner. It may mean nothing to you but basically in yachting terms it was bloody fast. Richard Beales owned the boat, an ex world champion dinghy sailor with Bob Fisher as crew so any dinghy sailors or readers of Yachts and Yachting amongst you will know how long ago this was.

We had been imbibing on a new friend's yacht when we were asked to introduce ourselves.

Robin, Dick, Mickey, Little Dave and Richard Beales. 'Richard Bilge you say' said our slightly deaf host, 'that will do' we all replied being that the Bilge is the lowest part of the boat. Poor Richard has been saddled with that nick name ever since.

Local Hero II

Anyway we had a great race up coast, one of those hot sunny clear blue days that never happen on a weekend, and we did well. After celebrating in the smart yacht club, refurbished after some brawl apparently, we lurched into town for a fish and chip supper. Bilge took a liking to a picture of a trawler man braving a stormy sea. Later we managed to stop him hurling a brick at the glass and nicking it. It's surprising what eight pints of Adnams does to you. The picture was about twenty foot square so how he expected to get it back on a thirty foot boat beats me.

We decided to search out the fleshpots or should that be fish pots of Lowestoft and found a disco. We were surprised as well.

Inside the club people were dancing the military two step, no it wasn't that bad in fact after a few more pints the girls started to look positively attractive. A couple of the crew pulled some woman on the dance floor whilst Alan and I propped up the bar. After a few taunts he disappeared into the gloom where he had seen an attractive filly but came back damn quick rubbing his face.

'The bitch smacked me' he blubbed into his beer, 'what did you say to her'? We asked, 'it was nothing I said, she's got a wooden leg and thought I was taking the piss'. 'Give it another try we chorused' this should be worth watching we thought as off he went.

Bursting onto the floor danced Vasco Da Gama Jones the well known Essex navigator with Mrs Long John Silver hanging gamely on, it nearly stopped the show.

'Don't be late boys' said Bilge as he fell out of the club, 'we've got another race tomorrow'!

In the morning I woke up and realised I wasn't in my bunk on the boat. How did I come to this conclusion, well there were curtains, it was a double bed and there was someone else in it. 'Morning' I said and shook hands with my companion, a tad formal you may say as we were both bollock naked, but my Mum had brought me up right.

'Shit, look at the time, we'll miss the race and where are we'? 'You're in Southwold' informed my companion and your mate sounds like he's still busy. Admittedly my mate hadn't been getting much at home for awhile but a race is a race. 'Come on mate' I shouted 'we've got to go', 'Oh shit' I heard him mutter as we dashed out of the house into one of the girls car who kindly drove us back to the marina.

Sitting all by herself gently rocking to her lines was Local Hero, in the distance the race fleet was just starting. The atmosphere on board was icy, Bilge was furious, the other boys more interested in how we had got on. 'Come on' I shouted 'the race has only just started if we sail out of here we won't have broken the race rules let's give it a go'. So up the boys jumped hoisted the sails and sailed out of the harbour crossing the start line some thirty minutes late, which surprised the race committee. We took an inshore flyer, which paid off and came in third thank God.

Bilge hadn't been exactly good the previous night either. On his way back to the boat he had missed his footing and fallen twenty feet into the harbour between two boats just avoiding a nasty injury. Little Dave always thought Bilge should be in a wheel chair due to his advancing years. He bought Bilge brake blocks for every birthday and would compliment him every morning on making it through another night. And so ended another quiet weekend on the sunny East coast.

Cupids little arrows had started to fly between Alan and Richards sister Judy so to help things along we invited them to join a crowd of us on a villa holiday in Corfu, one of two villas owned by an impoverished Socialist MP!

After a week of soaking up the sun and Ouzo, for some reason we hired a small boat, packed some food and wine, bought some charcoal and sailed off around the island. Finding a little secluded bay Alan roared into action, I think he was some distant relative of Baden Powel as he constructed shelters from driftwood and built a BBQ.

We eat and drank the night away and slept on the beach. Alan and Judy slipped away and found time for romance under the brilliant Mediterranean star filled sky. I woke early and kicked the ashes to get a pot of coffee on the go. Looking up the beach I could just see by the pale amber light of the creeping dawn Alan and Judy lying just near the tide line.

In the distance a fine white cruise liner was making her way up coast her wake shimmering behind her. Ten minutes later the wake reached the shore washing Alan and Judy up the beach. That will cool his ardour I thought!

I was their best man, and on another holiday in Greece was there at the conception, well nearly, of the first of their two beautiful daughters.

Well if all that nonsense doesn't get them to buy this book I'll be a Dutchman's uncle!

Hello Uncle Hertz van Rental I've just heard my nephew say.

Arse in a sling

I was peacefully driving back down the M1 towards Brentwood when a stab of pain shot through my lower spine. This feels familiar I thought, just like the arse problem in Mombasa so I drove straight to the doctor. The same abscess was diagnosed and off I was rushed to Harold Wood hospital for yet another excavation of my nether regions.

I awoke after the operation to see an apparition, I thought I had died and gone to the lounge bar in the sky, there administering to me was this beautiful oriental nurse.

When I came too in the morning I was in this long ward right at the end near the emergency exit. It looked like a second world war RAF Nissan hut and knowing the state of the health service it probably was. I scanned all the nurses, pretty as they were in that don't you love a woman in uniform and I wonder if they are wearing suspenders kind of way, none of them were from the East. Two were from Bethnal Green but that doesn't count.

I asked the guy in the next bed about the vision, 'you mean Vicki, she's the night nurse but she doesn't come on until eleven' he said. Now this posed a problem as all those of you who have spent time in hospital will know. Basically at six am when you are fast asleep they wake you up to give you a wash, a bed bath if you're lucky and some sort of gruel called breakfast. At about eleven you get another colour gruel called lunch then Doctors come and prod you and just as you are drifting off for an afternoon nap they wake you up for dinner. Lights are off by eight pm and its time for more kip.

'It's still the middle of the bloody day for Christ sake, how can I meet the night nurse if I'm supposed to be asleep'?

Vicki was an angel, the really sick patient's faces would light up when she spoke to them, but she kept her distance from me. It was only when I saw my medical clipboard that I understood. I had thought while they're doing my bum perhaps they could check out my other bits, well I had been a long time at sea. I didn't realise they would put check for venereal diseases in print, no wonder she always wore gloves when changing my dressings.

What also didn't help was the sight and sound of Ray and Gary two sailing pals walking down the ward carrying bags that clinked and the three of us being found comatose in the afternoon sun outside the emergency exit.

But this boy doesn't give in easily and within a month I had moved into Harold Wood nursing home.

Vicki was just beautiful in a delicate Malaysian way but not only in looks, her very soul shone with love and honesty. Critically sick patients at Broomfield hospital where she moved to be near our new home in Chelmsford would hang on to their thread of life just to say goodbye to her before they slipped away. There was not one ounce of badness in that girl and I am truly sorry that I treated her so badly.

We decided to have a holiday in Malaysia, as she hadn't seen her parents in many years. They lived on the mainland in a tiny village in or should it be on a house on stilts. Her father was the local schools English teacher, her mother spoke no English. Vicki was going home early to spend some time with her folks so she introduced me to her brother who was to meet me in Kuala Lumpur and look after me for a day before putting me on a plane to Penang. Sure I'll remember him I thought, oriental eyes, big glasses, black hair, yeah I'll recognise him. Arriving in Kuala Lumpa I discovered all Malays looked the same so I sat in the bar and let him find me.

The Malays are beautiful people, kind, gentle, very friendly with a mischievous sense of humour, I loved them. I was taken around loads of relatives all who had the strange idea that white men drank all the time so on arrival I was plied constantly with booze. I had brought a bottle of Johnny Walker black label scotch as a present for Vicki's dad, the Orientals love their whisky.

On our first night as a treat we went to a restaurant inside a refrigerated container, it was the only cool place in the village. One of the kids was dispatched to get the scotch, which her dad and I drank like wine all through the meal. Later as I lay on my dunlopillow in the spinning stilted house listening to the cries of the jungle monsters, I wondered where is the loo? Remembering it was at the bottom of their land next to the river I crossed my legs and fell asleep.

At six the next morning I went to the market perched on the back of her Dads Honda 50, with naked kids running beside me laughing and pointing at my fair hair which they'd never seen before. I ate breakfast with the Dad in the market place covering the food with very hot chilli sauce to hide the taste as frog, snake and rat were the day's specials.

We had a fabulous holiday, which stared my love affair with Malaysia and Thailand. We were visiting some Thai relatives when the military decided it was their turn to rule so we escaped on a very old and decrepit bus. I shared a seat with a little old lady her pig and a goat, interesting people actually. The loo a hole at the back of the bus was also quite interesting reminding me of old 'chippies' thunder box.

Back home in England Vicki's dinner parties were always oversubscribed, her delicate Malaysian cooking just overawed your taste buds, all this cooked on a two burner stove in my tiny cottage in Springfield on the outskirts of Chelmsford.

I must have spent too long in the pub before I bought the bloody place it wasn't built of brick but sponge. I'm not saying it was wet but when it rained we went and stood in the back garden, it was dryer there. It did have central heating one of those calor gas fires stuck in the middle of the lounge.

If you stepped out of the front door you would end up on a fast moving juggernaut on your way to Braintree. Dad eventually nailed a ton of plywood over the damp bits and found another fresh out of a pub prat who bought it.

With the few pennies it raised I became the proud owner of a 'Barrats Box' at the top end of Burnham on Crouch in Hermes drive, which was quickly tagged Herpes drive. I planted some Leylandi fir trees to provide privacy from the neighbours. Some twenty years later I popped back to look at the house and couldn't find it. Where it used to be was a forest of giant swaying fir trees, the poor bastards couldn't have seen any sun for decades so I quietly snuck away.

Work was going well, Bosch had brought in a specialist on compaction equipment called Wacker Jack. Wacker was our main competition as we had brought out a range of range of vibrating compaction plates and rammers. What with vibrators, plates and rammers I sounded like a regular member of S and M parties.

You must remember the Paddy's pogo stick. In any trench you would find Paddy struggling with a tube shaped thing with a two-stroke petrol engine at one end and a mud flattener at the other. Patrick would thump the thing down, bang went the engine up went the machine and then down to flatten the soil or his foot if he got it wrong. The new machines did that twice a second so far more effective unless they were yellow and had Bosch written on them in which case the engine would sulk and refuse to start.

I did once sell a vibrating plate to a hire company but on ringing back a week later to see how it was doing I was disconcerted to find it had caught fire on its first outing. Perhaps I should have sold him a Nu Swift fire extinguisher as an accessory!

We went to Frankfurt to visit Baulmer, which was a huge open-air exhibition of construction equipment, anything from a spade to gigantic earthmoving machines. The star of the show was a colossal machine with a front bucket, which could hold fifty people in it just to demonstrate its size. They filled it with scantily clad buxom German wenches and lifted them high in the air.

All around their stand the competitors with smaller machines looked glumly on. There was a loud bang as a hydraulic pipe broke, then like a dying dinosaur the bucket slowly fell to the floor spraying its life blood oil all over the watching throng and the buxom wenches. I had never seen a wet hydraulic oil T-shirt competition before. Gleefully all the competitor's machines burst into action, buckets going up and down and round and round, a very satisfactory sight!

Scramble

Bosch was heavily into exhibitions especially on their home soil. The Cologne hardware fair is probably the largest power tool exhibition in the world held in the massive Messe on the banks of the Rhine. People travel from all over the world to visit the show and to take in the sights of the historic city of Cologne with its centrepiece the magnificent Dom Cathedral.

The Bosch stand was the size of half a football pitch, over one hundred Bosch personnel mainly from Europe manned the stand and how about this in the middle was a restaurant for our customers run by very nubile students from the local university.

There was a Bosch committee that spent all year organising and designing the stand which cost in excess of three million DM and don't forget in addition was all the flights, hotels and living expenses of all the stand staff and yes we did fiddle these as well,.

British power tool exhibitions were a bit low key except for Hirex, which was the hire industries show, well more three day piss up really. It was held in the Wembley conference centre at the same time as the Benson and Hedges snooker tournament. After they had played you would often see the stars staggering about the show. My favourite was Hurricane Higgins who always stopped for a chat and would buy you a beer in the bar later and on one memorable evening shared some of his groupies with the lads and me.

Some senior wallah at Bosch decided we should run a competition for our dealers and the winners would be taken to the Cologne fair, winners being the customers who spent the most money with us.

There is such a huge influx of people at the major exhibitions that Rhine Cruisers, those long narrow passenger ships, are sailed down to Cologne and moored along the riverbanks in the centre of town to meet the demand for hotel beds.

We met the lucky winners at Heathrow and flew off to sample the dubious delights of Cologne. Leading the Bosch crew was Ron who I should tell you was a bomber pilot during the war and later went on to fly Vulcan's the delta wing bombers before joining Bosch. Terry an escapee from Kango and me plus the old hand Ron should be enough to control this lot I thought naively. This was the first trip for me with a bunch of so called business men, little did I know they were just as keen to get pissed up and laid as any other red blooded English men.

We taxied to the Rhine boats in immaculate latest model Mercedes. Why is it the world over taxi drivers think they are all Michael Schumacher's, I don't care how long it takes to get to the boat just get me there safely please Ralph or Michael, and what is German for slow the fuck up, bitter.

After booking into their berths we met our customers in the bar and took them for a tour of the city. Old Cologne has a maze of cobbled streets filled with bars and restaurants, well it's really not that old as Ron's mates dropped a fair amount of explosives on it back in the forties.

The Dom Cathedral took centuries to build and is worth a visit just to stand in the middle and gaze up at the towering dome and stained glass windows. They built the main railway station right next to the Dom and it is said that the RAF with precision bombing obliterated the station and only chipped the church.

What about St Paul's my German friends!

After feeding our guests copious German beers all at our cost as is the way in business, we took a lift to the top of the 711 tower to a restaurant with stunning views over the floodlit city.

There to meet us and to be our hosts were Bosch personnel from head office in Stuttgart who welcomed us warmly. After a fine meal, wine and buckets of brandy one of our German hosts asked Ron whether he had ever been to Cologne before.

Taking one of his slow puffs of his pipe Ron surveyed the city below him and replied, 'yes actually, some years ago and roughly at this altitude'. It went clean over our host's head, in fact the German sense of humour is so poor unless you hit them in the face with a custard pie or a frankfurter they will never see the joke.

Some of the more lively guys wanted to see more of the nightlife so Ron took the sad ones home and we hit the streets. Ron had thrust a wad of Deutsche marks into my hand and said give them a good time.

At three in the morning I herded my flock of drunks up the gangplank and into their cabins. For those slightly worse for wear the sanitary arrangements on the boat came into their own, as they were shall we say compact.

If you sat on the loo you could have a shit, throw up in the sink and wash your feet in the shower simultaneously, clever eh!

At half three in the morning I heard a knock on the door accompanied by a loud moan and a low voice saying, 'help me I'm dying'. Thinking it was a ruse for another drink I shouted 'you've had enough go to bed'. The moaning continued so I go out of bed to find one of my guests' prostrate on the corridor floor and yes he did have a funny colour. 'Wait here I'll get some help' I shouted running up the alleyway towards Ron's cabin, he'll know what to do being ex service and all that. After five minutes of banging and shouting scramble, your spitfires ready and other nonsense I realised Ron was out of it so I went and knocked up the night porter.

Full of German efficiency he called an ambulance and soon the green at the gills guest and me were tearing through the deserted streets siren wailing and blue lights flashing furiously.

Our man was rushed away on a stretcher while I dealt with the paperwork, which entailed me saying Bosch, it was like a magic wand, 'no problems sir' the duty nurse said. Half an hour later as dawn was breaking a Doctor approached and said the casualty had suspected appendicitis and that they should operate, only did I have his next of kin details so they could get permission to go ahead. 'I don't have them with me' I said 'but I have the information on the boat'.

So back I went in the ambulance a little more sedately this time and without the siren. Back on board after a while of rummaging I found his wife's details and started my way back to the hospital. As I went up the gangplank I was amazed to see the patient striding down it. 'Wait a minute you're supposed to be dying' I said. A chastened look came over his face, 'look I was pissed last night so I couldn't tell you, I drank far too much German brandy, which always gives me heartburn'.

'Oh bloody marvellous' I said 'I've been up all night trying to save you'. 'Never mind your problems 'he rejoined 'what am I going to tell the wife'. 'Say nothing she'll never find' out I bluffed. 'Oh yeah' he said 'so how do I explain that the nurses prepared me for the op', looking at my blank expression he added 'they fucking shaved me, my meat and two veg are as bald as a badger'.

Good point I thought, you go away to Germany on a business trip and come back with shaved nether parts, I often wonder what he told his wife.

Later that day our guests wandered around the massive halls in amazement at the size and sheer numbers of the power tool stands and especially at Bosch which was of course the biggest and busiest. Some went off looking for the British power tools, which they eventually found in a dark corner, tiny in comparison to Bosch, AEG, and the American giant Black and Decker.

It was a sign of the times that British manufacturing was falling behind the fast developing Eastern companies. Makita the Japanese newcomer already had wider ranges of competitively priced tools.

When I joined Bosch we had a turnover in the UK of one million pounds and about five % market share. Wolf the established British brand had the lions share with Kango hammers the builder's friend dominating construction and the hire industry. Black and Decker had the DIY market completely sewn up with no competition.

Within a few years Wolf stopped manufacturing, Kango's dominance declined as their ageing hammer range was replaced by superior products from Makita and Hitachi.

Decline and fall

In many areas British products failed to compete, outmoded designs, tiny budgets for research and development with the slogan buy British rapidly becoming why British?

For many years we had rubbished far Eastern products, Jap crap, Hong Kong plastic we chorused, so if you can't buy British buy German engineered products. This was in part true but the Japanese were also making good products and for a much lower price.

Take the British motor bike industry for example.

I had a Fanny Barnet 125cc, slow, unreliable and about as sexy as Andrew Lloyd Webber. My mate had a Suzuki 50, electric start, fast as hell and it started every time. I then bought a second hand Royal Enfield which to give it is due was fairly racy but no match for the high revving stomach kicking Kawasaki's, Yamaha's and Honda's, I rest my case. The rest is history except for sporadic attempts by some Brits to save the industry, Triumph was one case I think but now they have all gone.

You'll note the 'I think' in the last line. It's to stop any motor bike anorak writing to tell me the complete history of the Birmingham Small Arms company, I'm just drawing a parallel, making a point, Oh what's the use.

When I was in India a few years ago I was delighted to find new Royal Enfield's buzzing about built in some local factory and they still looked the same bless them.

Car radios, televisions, cameras, Hi Fi's all have succumbed to the Japanese. Mind you they still can't design a decent car interior.

In my sailing world long before marinas reared there ugly heads we all lay on moorings or anchored for the night. To get ashore to sample the local ale we jumped into the dinghy usually a clinker built scow and more latterly an Avon inflatable and rowed or sculled if you could remember how, ashore.

If you were posh you had an outboard motor, usually a British Seagull, which to be kind to it was fairly agricultural, to push you to the pub.

Just like motor bikes the Japanese have revolutionised outboard motor design and the British Seagull is now just a fond memory.

I was sitting in 'The Last Resort' a bar in the British Virgin Islands recently listening to the entertainer Tony Snell, a sort of mixture of Spike Milligan and Noel Coward, as he sang a British Seagull calypso to an audience of bemused American charterer's.

Tony takes great delight in taking the piss out of our American cousins and has done so for the last thirty years, they have absolutely no idea what he is singing about.

I thought of this scenario last night as the good ship Wizzo ploughed her lonely furlough through the dark Atlantic Sea.

Supposing an American came into an outboard motor shop desperate for a motor and the salesman had one last British Seagull on his shelf and his boss was equally desperate to get rid of it.

It could go something like this.

Salesman. 'Good morning sir how can I help you'.

American. 'My godamn motherfudding son of a bitch outboard blew up on me and Mary Lou wants to go water skiing today can you help me'?

Salesman. 'Certainly sir, we have a range of outboards to suit all manner of needs, though I should tell you we have something a little special which a connoisseur like yourself might be interested in, its British'.

American, 'Gee I love the way you British speak, kinda purty, tell me more boy'

Salesman 'Well it's called a British Seagull so bags of tradition, they have been built from the original design for over twenty five years, I hear Charley boy ran Camilla out to the royal yacht using one of these'.

'It runs on petrol, admittedly you have to throw in a bit of oil to make it run sweet but anyway you crack open this little silver screw thing to vent air from the tank then grope around under here to find the fuel tap, horizontal for on, upright for off'.

American. 'Seems pretty straight forward so far boy'.

Salesman. 'Right, then do a bit more groping to find this disc shaped thing that operates the choke. You have to shut it when it's cold and open it when the engines hot although sometimes you do it the other way round depending how the engine feels at the time. Now this is the bit I like and it's a design feature none of your modern engines have'.

American. 'What that stick with a bit of sting through it with a knot on the end'.

Salesman. 'Yes sir we call it the starting rope, you wrap it around this groove on the top of the engine making sure the knot is held in this notch but not too tightly as, well I'll come back to that later. Pull briskly but not too hard we don't want to see sir bum in air do we Ha Ha, and the engine will burst into life and immediately propel you forward'.

American. 'What about the clutch'?

Salesman. 'Well that's the beauty of the design, no heavy clutch or clumsy gear levers just start and go and when you want to go in reverse just swing the whole thing around and backwards bound you are. Just a word of advice best not to wear a tie as the flywheel does rather attract them'.

American 'Gee it sounds rather fun'.

Salesman 'Well you could follow the herd and buy a Yamaha four stoke electric start easy transmission forward and reversed geared Enduro but where's the fun in that'.

American. 'I'll take the Seagull'

Sales man. 'An excellent choice sir, by the way tell Mary Lou to run down the beach with her skis on to give the engine a sporting chance'.

UKOBA

I shouldn't take the piss out of the old British Seagull, thousands of mariners have sworn by or should that be sworn at the damn things as despite frequent dunking in the briny they just keep on going. Later models did have clutches and covered in flywheels but I think they lost its soul when they made those modifications.

A few years ago a pal named Danny rang me up and invited me to motor across to Calais on his Hardy motor boat. It was not a plastic fandango, more a solid seaworthy work boat so I readily accepted. The last motor trip with Danny had been in the depths of winter from Burnham to Tower Bridge but that's another story.

Actually it bears a telling. It was a late December evening with snow in the wind, Danny's boat sat to its mooring lines at the end of the Royal Burnham's pontoon. We had planned a delivery trip out of the river hopping the sand banks of Foulness into the Thames and upriver under Tower Bridge to the boats new home. As the weather was inclement we took in a curry and thoughts turned to a night cap. Danny trained in from London with a VIP and ordered us to make way. Trudging through a blizzard leaving sailing boot imprints in the virgin snow we boarded and cast off. The radar played an important part of the trip as the visibility was nil. Steaming along in the darkness with the cabin heater up high and a convivial glass of scotch in hand one by one the crew dropped off, not a clever thing to do as we threaded our way through the busy shipping channels. In the morning our little snow clad vessel cut a fine swathe through the brilliant winter sunshine past the Thames barrier and under the London bridges, a memorable trip.

Anyway back to the Calais adventure. On this

occasion we were to be joined by George Kingston an Essex butcher and Big Dave who lent me the big yank car to upset the girl friends parents many years before and is still a good friend today.

The forecast wasn't particularly good but the boat was well found so off we set. Barrelling through rolling seas the hardest worker on the trip was the windscreen wiper as we sat in the cabin warmth supping hot beverages.

We made Calais by late afternoon and as is often the way the wind quietened and the sun shone as we nosed into the heart of the docks. Passing the sailing club we noticed they were flying more than the usual national flags of nearby countries. The biggest flags had the logo UKOBA on them, which puzzled us, Lamborghini, Ferrari and Porsche were also represented.

After a brief stop at a local café to get the flavour of the land i.e. drinks some local beer we set off for the club.

It was empty save for some worried looking men in reefers talking on the phone and studying weather faxes. The whole room was set out for a prize giving, rows and rows of tacky looking trophies each one with one of those racing driver laurels around them. Of more interest were some other tables stacked with champagne filled ice buckets.

'Are you with UKOBA' said one harassed looking official, the obvious answer, 'no I'm with the Woolwich' probably wouldn't have gone down well. 'No' said Danny 'we have just motored across from Burnham'.

Suddenly we were surrounded, 'motored you say' said another official, 'wasn't it rough'?

'Nothing that an old Hardy can't handle' bragged Danny.

You must join us for a drink, so we set too and though I say it myself made a fairly respectable dent in the champers. 'By the way what's this shindig all about, what does UKOBA stand for'? Asked George.

'Well it's the United Kingdom Offshore Boating Association, a fleet of boats are racing from Tower Bridge to here only the weathers too rough for them' replied one of the guys.

Poor little power boat people we thought as we helped ourselves to more grog.

'Best of luck' we hailed as we fell out the door, 'hope they get here tomorrow'. After a fine dinner in one of our favourite haunts we retired to bed, it had been a long day.

A bright breezy morning greeted us as we had breakfast in one of those little pavement cafes. Replete with croissants, coffee and an early morning livener we set off to do the town. George affected the bohemian look. He had one of those leather handbags so loved by the Spanish; hanging off his wrist by its strap giving him what he thought was a rakish air. Personally I thought he looked like a poof! I have a wonderful photo of George and Big Dave looking furtive under a café awning emblazoned with the words Le Liaison Dangerous, Danny said they could have been mistaken as a pimp and his minder!

'Let's check out the yacht club' said Dave so off we trolled to find no change, still empty. Drinks were pressed into our hands again as we were informed that due to the weather all the racers were coming across by ferry to receive their prizes.

Now that's the type of racing I could aspire to. You get the before race piss up, have a good night's sleep, leave your boat snug in harbour and jump a ferry. I suppose you would have to enjoy a fine lunch on board, disembark, and make your way to the yacht club, collect your prizes, have some champagne and ferry back. One flaw, how do you know who's won?

I suppose you could have a race from the ferry to the club. Maybe a three-legged one by tying a sail tie around your legs, no that wouldn't work motorboats don't have sail ties. I know an egg and spoon race now that would really make the sports page of the Telegraph.

Fate had one more card to play, the rough seas outside Calais had held up the ferry docking so it wasn't until late afternoon the racers arrived. To a man they all wore those shiny leather effect sporty jackets, baseball hats with loads of scrambled egg on the peak and whoever had sponsored them splashed across their backs.

The girls were all blonde, legs up to their armpits, huge dark sunglasses, a slash of vivid red lippy, tight, tight white ankle length slacks and high heel shoes you could bungee jump off. Of more interest were the scantily clad serving girls wearing bright red Ferrari, or brilliant yellow Lamborghini jackets.

They soon tucked into an orgy of food and drink whilst we tried to mingle. Some prat in a hat cornered me and said 'who's your sponsor' and I'm glad to say it gave me great pleasure to reply, 'British Seagull' and as we turned to leave I added, 'long shaft'. Spilling ourselves out of the club we boarded our tidy craft and barrelled our way back to 'Blighty'. Not a bad run up the road we all agreed.

Jeep Drivers Bum

Bosch had promoted me to Business Development manager with a team of three guys to investigate new areas of commerce to sell power tools. We were still handcuffed to our distribution network of about forty five wholesalers who sold to the general dealers, hardware stores, hire companies, farming outlets and the like. I started to speak to the big builder's merchant chains, Travis Perkins, Jewson's and Plumb Centre, in fact anywhere builders, electricians, 'chippies' went to buy power tools.

My old mates Rick and Brian from the old Southern area would still meet for a drink as I tried to find promotion for them. We had been through a lot together including a few grab a granny nights. Rick and I borrowed the National Sales Managers giant Ford Zodiac for a couple of weeks and roared around London looking like Reagan and Carter until the prat realised his car was missing.

Derek was his name, a very poor employment decision, but he did give us some laughs. He ordered me to meet him at Shaw's, a dealer on the Purley Way in Croyden, one Monday at ten in the morning. I was living with Ingrid a German girl at Sidcup at the time so Croydon with the rush hour was at least two hours. The Northern prat was staying at Luton so I advised he either left very early or allow four hours. Of course he knew better, it was only fifty miles as the crow flies he reasoned, and tried to drive through central London. Apparently he arrived way after lunch by which time I had secured the order and gone home.

He lasted a very short time until Bosch management saw through him and he was on his way.

I had some more medical problems so after a visit to the doctor I was sent to Broomfield hospital for more tests. Do not eat for twenty-four hours before your appointment said the letter. When I eventually found Out Patients I was ushered into a room with two old biddies sitting behind a big shiny machine with lots of dials, gauges, valves and pipes. 'Take your clothes off in the changing room and put on the medical gown' they ordered.

When I got back they asked me to turn around and bend over. Well I have done my fair share of mooning but never in front of two old dears. As I bent over they peered up my rectum, tutted and appeared to be in disagreement. 'I think he's a C' said one, 'no definitely a B' replied the other.

'This won't hurt' they said, now whenever I hear those words I know it's going to hurt like hell. Some sort of lubricant was applied to a nozzle thing and inserted sharply up my arse. When my feet returned to the floor and my howl had stopped echoing around Chelmsford they agreed I probably was a B after all. The nozzle was changed and in it went. 'This might tickle a bit' they said, see above.

Now I know colonic irrigation has its devotees in the fashion world but to me being pumped full of water through your arse is not top of my list of pleasurable pastimes. As my stomach heaved and ballooned the girls said 'you will probably want to use the loo when we disconnect' and they were right, I only just made it!

Next stop was to go and see the consultant, so little gown on I padded down the corridor and knocked on an impressively big wooden door. 'Come' said an authoritative voice, so I walked into this room full of what I presumed were medical students. A white coated distinguished looking gent said 'hello Mr Tickner please go into that room, remove your gown and lay face down on the examination table'. So off I went into that room and lay there arse in the air with some trepidation.

They all crowded into the room behind me, I hoped the big boil on my right buttock had cleared up, but worse was to come.

'Winston please hold Mr Tickners buttocks apart' requested the consultant, glancing around I saw this big black guy parting my cheeks, 'and Mary please insert the octoscope'. Mary was drop dead gorgeous and she was going to look up my arse, in fact they all did, what a way to make a living! When they pulled the periscope thing out it felt just like passing a motion, Oh no I thought, they all are looking at my arse with a steaming turd coiled neatly by my balls. Thankfully I remembered the old girls had flushed me through so panic over.

They then strapped me to a machine that turned me upside down and around and around to take X-rays, I won't bother with funfairs again.

A letter arrived next week to say they had found nothing. Later that week however that old familiar feeling at the base of my spine came back and I was rushed into hospital with the old abscess problem yet again.

Waking up after the op in Broomfield Hospital I was in a general ward, but I'm with BUPA I thought as the elderly gentleman in the next bed lost his fight with his bedpan. A crash of pan on floor, a moan as the old boy followed it and off they slid down the ward lubricated by the bed pans contents. I'm with BUPA I thought again, I should be in a private ward and lapsed back to sleep.

In the morning the consultant a Mr something or other followed by his entourage of doctors, nurses and students stopped at my bed. 'This is Mr Tickner who has Jeep driver's bum' explained the Mr pausing for the expected laughter from his minions. I butted in, 'actually it was Vauxhall Cavalier arse', which didn't go down well. 'Anyway' he blustered 'this is the third time Mr Tickner has had this operation so we have taken drastic measures this time and he will be testing out some new medication'. With that and with a twirl of his stethoscope he and his party moved on to their next victim. I didn't like the sound of he will be testing new medication, what happened to the guinea pigs?

They called it jeep drivers bum because the seats in jeeps were uncomfortable and pushed in at the bottom of the spine. This could cause hairs to bend and grow into your lower back. Sweat running down your back would enter the body thus poisoning the abscess.

If some smart arse Doc has a better explanation then good all I know it's bloody painful and I don't wish it on any one, except for the bastard that clamped me recently.

A couple of days after the 'op' I was taken into a side room, stripped and put in a big round bath with a pull switch hanging above it. A pretty shiny black nurse, all smiles and teeth gave strict instructions. I was to let the hot water soak and soften the half a mile of wadding in my wound and then when I felt strong enough I was to slowly pull it out. Any problems then just pull the cord and I'll come and help, giving me a reassuring smile she pulled the door shut behind her.

Well this is a fine to do I thought as I gently started pulling. After about half an hour I had about two hundred yards of pink wadding washing about my knees in water that had a very reddish tinge to it. Now I can't stand the sight of blood especially my own so I pulled the cord. The light went out and wouldn't come back on no matter how much I pulled the damn cord. I sat there in darkness thinking what a great place to bleed to death so I pulled myself out and crawled to the wall and felt for the door. Eventually I found it and painfully eased myself straight into the main ward crying pitifully for a nurse.

Unfortunately it was by now visiting hour and the ward was full of relatives, mistresses and friends. I must have cut quite a dash crawling across the floor buck naked with a mile of red wadding hanging out my arse.

I was moved to a private ward after that.

My pal Gary's wife Carole picked me up and took me home sitting on an inflatable ring, boy was I sore.

My house in 'Herpes Drive' was a stone's throw from the medical centre to which I was to report each morning for treatment. Bosch were very understanding and said only come back when you are fully recovered.

The first morning I hobbled round doing one of those I think I've shit myself type walks and was sat down in the waiting room on my little rubber ring much to the amusement of one little boy or swine as I would prefer to call him.

After reading all the latest Country Life's, did you know you can make an omelette from powdered egg and how sad the King has died, I was eventually called to see the Doctor. Standing besides the great man was a pretty nurse holding a medical bowl containing shiny steel implements presumably to remove my dressings.

'Ah Mr Tickner' he said 'welcome' I'm really looking forward to this, your report says they undertook some radical surgery'. 'Please call me Robin' I said, 'I think you are going to get to see quite a lot of me', and if by radical you mean painful you are spot on the dot.

'Capital, capital' he beamed, 'now let's have taken a look, just drop your trousers and lean on the bed'. So once more I was bending over showing my arse to a strange man, 'my God' he exclaimed 'they didn't bugger about did they', his words were accompanied by a deep sigh from the nurse and a clatter of surgical steel as she keeled over in a dead faint.

'You could get your whole fist in there' he murmured, well I had heard of fisting and my arse was in no fit state to stand any of that nonsense. The nurse groggily got to her feet and handed the Doc some new instruments to remove the final two miles of wadding. 'What's this new treatment they were talking about' I asked hoping it was less painful then my previous experiences.

'Oh right', said the Doc excitedly, 'it's brand new and you're the guinea pig', thanks I thought, just what I need. 'You see you have two pots of chemicals which you mix together and pour in the wound. The reaction forms a foam rubber blob which fits the contours of your wound thus preventing bacteria to enter and your skin granulates', sensing my confusion, 'it grows from the inside out', he explained.

Each treatment should use less and less chemicals until it's totally healed and Bobs your uncle. Well I don't have an Uncle Bob but it sounded a lot less painful than packing my orifice with wadding. So each day I waddled round to have my two pot Polly treatment. There was one small hiccup I tended to leak a little so the Nurse wrote me a prescription for sanitary towels. As I explained in hushed tones my unusual request to the chemist, the other customer's thought I was shyly buying condoms but after a few days I got bolder. 'what sort of day are you having today Mr Tickner' the chemist would enquire with a conspiratal wink, 'oh heavy, light or medium' I would reply much to the confusion of the other shoppers. The packaging is all wrong on those ladies products, it states clearly I could play tennis and go horse riding. Well I know sod all about tennis except when I fell asleep in centre court pissed at a corporate hospitality day and I was hardly likely to go riding sitting on a rubber ring was I?

After a few days I was bored stiff so I rang Big Dave and said 'why don't we put some outriggers on my boat to make it go faster', 'but you've got your arse in a sling' he said.

'It's alright if I stand, I'll go mad sitting here watching the box'. 'You're on he said', Dave likes a challenge.

Fly Détente and Die happy

**Détente the boat Big Dave and I modified.
Burnham week 1995 crewed by Tickner's**

I had bought a very old Soling (three man Olympic sailing boat) from a pal who had discovered two behind the aircraft hangar at Calshot near Southampton. He built a little cuddy on it and raced her very successfully winning Burnham week and many other trophies.

Forgive me non-sailors perhaps you should read a few back copies of Yachts and Yachting to get a handle on this next bit.

I went to my local Barclays bank to get a loan as I had sod all in my account. 'Brian the bank' as he was known granted me an interview and greeted me warmly. 'How's the old man' he asked, I had forgotten Dad had worked with him many years ago. Sadly he had to refuse a loan due to the state of my account, 'what do you want it for' he asked as I went to leave his office.

'I want to buy a boat' I said, 'why didn't you say, of course we can help how much do you need'. I had also forgotten that Brian was a mad keen sailor so I got my boat.

A Soling is an open boat twenty four foot long and in its proper pristine form used to be raced in the Olympics and we did quite well in them.

I wanted to be outrageous, pile as much sail on as possible, fit wings, and go fast, speed to meet your need yahooooo.

I borrowed a mast and boom from a Sydney Harbour skiff those speed machines that race off the Sydney Opera house and got some giant sails cut.

Big Dave drove me carefully across to my parents house each day after my treatment and my assurances to the Doc that I was resting, to work on the boat. Détente sat on her trailer next to the folk's front wall on which we would balance precariously.

Dave measured, tutted, sawed and planed whilst I groaned and held bits of wood, nails and glue. Every now and then Mum came out with tea and sandwiches and later brandy as we froze in the November mists.

Slowly the boat came together; we painted the decks white and the hull that lovely racing blue, she looked a picture

Well the bum eventually healed, when I farted I no longer sounded like a two tone police siren so I went back to work.

In the spring I launched Détente and went on to win most feature races, the Wednesday night series and to top it all Burnham week, crewed fearlessly by Buster and any other lunatic speed freak. Buster had some fluorescent badges made up, fly Détente and die happy they shouted, boy was she fun. In any breeze with the kite up she lifted her bow and planed into the distance. Coming back on the wind was a different story, two crew sailed and one bailed to keep her afloat I felt a kindred spirit to those intrepid Cape Horner's.

She was also a bit of a babe magnet so I had a series of girl crews named imaginatively Bob one, two and three, Blackadder style. The sanitary arrangements were a little basic. Bob three, Mel got her arse stuck in the loo bucket one rather long Wednesday night race, she wouldn't now as she is just a stick of a girl.

Each Burnham week brothers Joff, Buster and sometimes to our delight Jeremy from Australia would crew which would be reported in the Yachts and Yachting as the brothers Tickner sailing their enigmatic flying machine Détente, oh happy days.

After the race we would moor up behind an old half tonner Lynx our main rival and drink copious amounts of Mick's gin. On one occasion we repaid their kindness by hosting our own party fixing spirit optics to Détentes coach roof with Mick's dory moored behind complete with bucket as the loo. The party nearly sank my poor little craft; it was supposed to hold three crew, not twenty three!

Détente Chelsea Pensioners! Me, Jeremy, Bob1, Buster and Joff doing his Benny Hill impersonation

Not only did we sail hard in the Burnham week regatta we also partied hard especially on review night. This was a night at the Crouch Yacht Club where frustrated singers and actors from many of the race boats would stand up on stage and well make fools of ourselves.

Many acts were so drunk they could hardly stand let alone sing; at least they were enjoying themselves unlike the bemused audience. For many years I had the pleasure to compere this feast of lunacy with many acts performed by the Tickner brothers and on occasions dear old Dad.

Sargeant Major Guy Tickner

My favourite was Dad as a slightly elderly sergeant

major drilling his troop of Chelsea Pensioners, Detente's crew sitting in chairs pretending to be in wheelchairs with all the attendant pretend wheel turning. You had to be there! I think Bob on the electric organ and the 'clapometer' had the most fun.

The Buckley Goblets

The East Anglian racing series consisted of weekly bashes around the sandbanks of the Thames estuary ending in a final dash across the North Sea usually in a howling gale in Mid September just in time to fill the boat up with duty free and hopefully to win the 'Buckley Goblets'.

Mick rang me up and said 'how do you and Ox fancy doing the 'Goblets', it's going to blow a gale so we stand a chance'. Lynx was a very heavy old fashioned boat that revelled in a breeze.

Ox and I fancied it a lot so joined the boat in a muddy creek called Bradwell ready to slip across the river in the morning for the start at West Mersea.

Mick had this brilliant idea, celebrate winning on the Thursday night just in case the wind was light, OK with us drank the crew. It was one hell of a party, Mick's gin and tonics are legendary, in fact all the way across the channel we heard the clinking of glasses around the boat where some poor sot had hidden his drink before collapsing unconscious. We fared badly in the race, partially because the wind was light and didn't suit Lynx being an elderly lady, but mostly because the crew were severely hung over. The good bit however was that we had recovered by the time we reached Ostende ready for a night up the road.

Ostende in those days did not boast a marina, there was a narrow pontoon all around the dock walls with mooring buoys scattered around the middle. The boats had to pick up a mooring and try to go stern too the pontoon, not an easy job in the dark with a gale blowing.

If you were late in, all the best spots were taken so you moored wherever you could find a space. Getting ashore was the next obstacle involving pulling boats together and leaping from vessel to vessel before reaching dry land. Add the extra frisson that the dock was full of the contents of all the boat loos and also a dumping ground for dead cats and dogs. This made jumping and not falling in a very important health issue.

If you don't believe me about the dead animals ask Gary Sims, he went in to free a snarled propeller and came up looking like David Crocket with a dead cat on his head as in the royal joke where's the fox hat?

First stop would be the North Sea yacht club to drink copious amounts of Euro piss or Belgium lager as its better known. I had discovered an alternative to prevent mind numbing lager hangovers. I drank Pernod and water. In the morning when you woke as the others reeled around you holding their cracking heads, I would drink some water and be pissed again so having a head start on the others when we went off for a liquid lunch in the town square.

After the club the crews went forth in search of fun, there were numerous dubious bars, discos, and even houses of ill repute. Often is the time we have lurched out of a drinking establishment into the glare of the hot morning sun and gone for a pavement café breakfast.

On this night however we ended up in a disco and John a fellow crew and I pulled, well it was more like rounded up actually as there was at touch of the bovine about our companions. John the swine was too quick for me and disappeared into the girl's hotel leaving me on the pavement with my new friend impatient for action. 'You've got a boat' she said accusingly 'let's get on it'. Lust overcame nausea so I extended an arm and we weaved off, Ermingtrude trotting faithfully besides me.

I remembered the crew wanted breakfast on board so I bought a loaf of bread at an early opening baker.

By now dawn was well under way and in its pale light I risked a glimpse of my companion. She was how should I put it large, no that's not it fucking huge, wearing a floral dress, black fish net stockings and high heels. How was I going to get this on board and why!

As we stepped on the dock she asked 'which boat was mine'. Pointing to Lynx in the distance she whinnied 'I'm game let's go'. Well I pulled them bloody boats together and game girl that she was she somehow got onto Lynx. On the way over holding grimly onto the stern of one boat the owner popped his head up. Dressed in natty pyjamas, he said 'need any help old boy' to which I replied in the negative. The loaf held between my clamped teeth dropped into the oily water, sod it.

Clambering on board Lynx I saw all the berths were taken except the one under the chart table which required a complete breakdown to access its comforts. Mick woken up by our arrival studied my companion and offered this advice; 'it's my considered opinion that unless you lever your friend in with a large crowbar she ain't going to fit'. She took umbrage at this and flounced off, thank God I thought as I collapsed in the cockpit.

Many years later when I first met Bilge he said 'weren't you the guy who ran that big bird in fishnet stockings over to Lynx'? So remember your past sins will always come back to haunt you.

In the afternoon the duty free would be delivered to the club providing you had remembered to order it the night before. A crackly loudspeaker system informed the boats that the goods were ready to collect.

There was a boat called 'Farthing', which was designed by Bruce Farr so the name was a play on words, Far Thing, which obviously went clean over the Belgium announcers head.

Over the speakers came this gem, "will the following boats please collect their duty free,' Fiona of Burnham, Lynx and wonderfully, Farting, will the Farting crew please collect her goods echoed around the dock.

Dad had taken on the task of support vehicle driver so he could enjoy drinking with our crew who loved Dad's eccentric ways. Tubby Lee, Burnham's rigger and infamous larrikin joined our crew. Tubby has crewed with 'Phil the Greek' and Edward Heath amongst many other notable sailors in an illustrious and very successful sailing career so we were delighted he adopted us. Many years later we would sit in the Mallorca sun supping beers in a marina bar reminiscing about the foolish things we did in our youth and still are actually.

On a later East Anglian race week we abandoned the muddy east coast of England and ventured further afield with Dover our first stop then onto Ostend and through the Dutch waterways. We had a wet race through the Goodwin Sands down to Dover to meet Dad who had set up camp with a more upmarket van. It had wind down stabilising jacks, a galley, comfy beds and a store for all of Tubby's rigging spares. As sailors do we found a local hostelry leaving Dad to rig a makeshift line to hang all our sopping wet sailing gear in a vain attempt to dry it before the next race. Some drinks later Dad joined us in the pub, breathing heavily, muttering something about bloody French truck drivers. Apparently he hadn't taken into account the height of French trucks in his drying line height so as he hung the last item up a juggernaut came round the corner and pulled the lot down. Father's breathlessness was explained by having to chase up the road to retrieve our gear. 'How far did you have to run asked Mickey' Well not that far' replied Dad 'your visibility is a bit reduced with half a ton of wet oilskins wrapped around the windscreen'. Yet another classic Dad tale, I wonder what the truck driver thought? On arrival in Ostend we found the van parked right outside the North Sea yacht club all jacked up on what appeared to be railway lines. After the usual celebrations we fell asleep to be awoken at three, well I never, by several very large Belgium policemen. 'Do you know you are parked on top of the dock railway lines and please can you move as a train is due soon' they politely requested. Dad beat us to the cab, gunned the engine then drove sedately to a safer parking spot. The whole effect was made more interesting by the shower of sparks shooting out from under the van lighting up the night sky. 'Perhaps you should have wound the jacks up' commented Tubby dryly. Dad followed us through Holland, always there with a case of beer to demolish in the yachts cockpit after a hard days racing and eager to yarn the night away with Tubby.

We were racing a class of boat called a Shamrock that season, thirty foot long, designed by Ron Holland and there was seven racing in the series. They went like a witch on the wind in the light but downwind in a blow you couldn't speak because you had your sphincter in your mouth. These boats would roll on a wet sponge.

Finishing yet another Ostende race in the dead of night, kite up, blowing a gale, decks awash the crew were all back aft tying to keep the rudder in the water so the struggling helmsman could steer. The last turning mark the Binnenstroom Bank buoy was illuminated by a one candlepower light which stood no chance of being seen against the lights of the shore, 'head for the casino' shouted Alan the navigator.

'I will if you stop gripping the life rails so bloody hard' hollered the skipper, 'the whites of your knuckles are spoiling my night vision'.

Another good run up the road followed, I think we won the Goblets. I know Dick held on to the precious casket all the way home. I believe due to the Pernod I was a little previous in going to sleep, in fact a large tureen of soup was my pillow and a restaurant my bedroom. A sharp rap on my head by a large waitress with the soup ladle brought me round and I was dispatched back to the boat in disgrace with Alan as my guide.

The fresh air revived me so I persuaded Alan to have a few pit stops on the way back to the boat, two of us in 'shit street' now I gleefully stumbled. When the crew arrived back, I was fully oil skinned and ready to cast off, a model crew, which lasted nearly ten minutes after we cleared the pier heads. When I awoke we were off the 'Longsand Head' nearly home with a not very happy crew seeing as I had missed two watches.

There was a stranger on board who had cadged a ride home, he was looking a bit sheepish and eventually whispered something into our skippers ear. Ox nodded sagely, 'guys' he said 'John here has admitted to having two bottles of duty free whisky on board and he is worried about customs'. 'He suggests we throw one overboard, what do you think'? Why don't we strain it first' suggested Alan. So we drank it and pissed it overboard, and while we were at it we drank the second bottle for good measure.

When the customs rummage squad pulled alongside, all smart and navy clad with lots of scrambled egg on their cap peaks they took one look at our slumped forms and the senior office muttered 'there's nothing for us here lads the bastards have drunk it all'!

All boats have a handicap, something to do with length, weight, sail area and whether you had slept with the measurer's daughter. Nobody ever thinks their handicap is fair which is why one design is so popular, whoever finishes first wins, simple really.

We were breezing along the Goodwin Sands home of hundreds of wrecks, even a German U boat pops its head up sometimes on the right low tide, with all the Shamrocks racing neck and neck. 'The kite won't come down' panicked our fore deck hand, 'send Tic up' shouted back the skipper. Foolishly I was the lightest so clipping on the bosun's chair I was hauled to the top of the mast and waited for instructions to break the snap shackle.

Carving great arcs in the sky I eventually howled 'shall I open the bloody thing'? A muffled answer came back up the mast, 'no hold on tight we're going faster with you up there'.

The Thames Estuary race took you out from Burnham around the banks and finished at Garrison point at the mouth of the Medway and we were winning. 'It's in the bag' one of the crew said which as you know is the kiss of death. It's never over until the fat lady starts singing and sure enough as we were just about to cross the line for an overall victory the wind shut off and the tide took us the wrong side of the buoy.

We frantically anchored to stop being swept even further away and sat there watching impotently as the fleet appeared over the horizon, noted our problem, tacked and finished. Eventually the tide slackened enough to allow us to cross the line. Our skipper Ox not noted to be of good temper, threw a winch handle on the deck in frustration which bounced high and disappeared into the briny, thus adding a twenty pound bill to his woes.

After the race you have to motor all the way up to Upnor for the après race piss up past the coal yards, power stations and general squalor of the Medway towns. To add to our misery we were hailed by a boat in distress and had to tow them all the way up the river halving our speed thus reducing valuable drinking time.

In the eighteenth century the Dutch Navy sailed up the Medway, fired some cannon shot at Upnor Castle and escaped unmolested, I wish they had tried harder and been more accurate.

On another occasion we raced a self built Humphries half tonner to the Medway and did quite well which meant more than the usual amount of liquor was consumed after mooring the boat and hitching a ride ashore.

There were two sailing sisters on the racing circuit both very pretty except one had a moustache!

Somehow I managed to persuade one, guess which, to come back to the boat for a nightcap, a euphemistic term for a legover. Hailing a bumboat we puttered back to Spirit, 'stay in the cockpit' I whispered 'I'll sort out a bed'. Racing boats, by the way, were stripped right out with very spartan accommodation to keep weight to a minimum.

Despite my desperate entreaties, offers of money or I'll even leave the light on so you can watch, the boys were as one and would not give up their bunks, even Little Dave asleep in the heads was a no go. Tiptoeing down below we fell out of our clothes and began to grapple on a four foot long by ten inches wide berth. It was covered with that special type of plastic that sticks to your arse and makes farting noises with an added bonus of a rigging strap fastened right in the middle.

Knowing full well that the boys were wide-awake and enjoying the cabaret we moaned and explored in stage whispers. 'You're so hunky' she breathed into my ear, I distinctly heard the muffled titters of the boys, but her next line, 'I knew the minute I saw you I had to have you' brought an explosion of laughter. I'm going for a pee she said huffily so the children can go to sleep. As Dave still had his head down the pan she went up top, dropped her bum over the life rails and relieved herself. Unfortunately she was in full view of Dick who muttered 'now that's my type of woman, thank you God' and fell back to sleep.

At dawn we jumped a passing boat to drop her back ashore to the surprise of my skipper who had just arrived, 'what was that' he asked, 'don't ask me' I said 'but it needed ironing'.

11 Chapel Rd

My Barrets box was proving too small for parties so following a long family tradition I bought a three storey terraced house in Chapel Rd. Father, Jonathan then me and Buster all had lived in this road. Why, well it was near the river, near Barclays bank and most importantly, the Star, the White Harte and the Anchor public houses were all within staggering distance.

'The house is a bit run' down' Big Dave and I commented as we stood in the front doorway. Stepping in Dave fell through the floor, 'and the floor is rotten' he added.

We set up an ambitious refurbishment plan which involved me getting back early from work for six months which wasn't a problem as mobile phones hadn't been invented so Bosch never knew where you were from week to week.

I employed Danny Brewer to do the proper building work and Dave and I were the labourers. There are not too many houses in Burnham that don't have some of Danny's work in or on them, mind it helps to be deaf and own a tea plantation as Dan will only work with his radio at full bore and a tea cup and fag in his hands.

When we pulled up the soaking wet floor we found the dividing wall rubble had just been dropped under the joists. I filled three skips with that rubbish collecting a hernia on the way. We replaced the staircase, we had to as I had got pissed and ordered a bath that wouldn't fit up the stairwell. I borrowed an old kitchen from my mate who was having a new one fitted and using my contacts at Bosch filled it with Bosch white goods.

Dick plastered the walls in the traditional Essex way, Big Dave fell over in the traditional Essex way and put his hand on the still wet plaster so we had to hang a picture pretty damn quick so as not to upset Dick.

The only room we left alone was Postman Pat's room. The previous owner had a kid so had decorated his room with everything made for that bloody postie. The wallpaper, light shade, duvet, even the carpet. Mickey Whitehead one of our long suffering crew members slept there and he reckons he had nightmares about Pats black cat, I think he was just dreaming of pussy. By the way what do they call Postman Pat when he retires? Pat!

We had some fabulous times in that house, after the club or pubs closed most of the village would find their way back for a nightcap, it was always open house. I or we used it for weekends and for Wednesday nights when I was racing. If walls had ears that house could tell a tale or two. In Burnham week it became a bunkhouse with bodies strewn all over the place, most of them people who couldn't find the front door to go home.

When I sadly sold it the estate agent asked for any spare front door keys. After a prolonged search I gave him twenty-four sets, it was that kind of open house!

I Get around

Just like the Beach Boys song my life seems to be always on the move, I was now staying in Carshalton, Surrey don't you know, with Karen a schoolteacher who was destined to be one of the youngest headmistresses in Essex. She was kind, fun loving and ever patient with me, putting up with my travelling all week around the country with work and gallivanting around the North Sea at weekends.

We had some great times together and yet again I wish I could turn back the clock and have looked after her better. She now lives in Burnham, happily married with a fine family and still has time to hug me with that concerned look of hers. Mum and Dad still get a Xmas card from her, she was always Dad's favourite.

Work was becoming even more competitive, distributors now stocked more and more brands and the Japanese were determined to be number one in the British market.

We had to budget more for free lunches and corporate hospitality. The Elcocks a fine Yorkshire family had most of the lunches, which may account for their girths but they did stock our tools, eventually.

We ran a series of clay pigeon shoots around the country. In the morning we would give a presentation on new products then an alcohol free lunch, we didn't want any accidents with guns amongst the guests. In the afternoon we knocked seven bells out of the clays, very satisfying, and due to the number of events, I became a reasonable shot.

When the competition copied us we tried motor racing.

All around Britain are race circuits the most famous I suppose being Brands Hatch in Kent. We followed a similar format, a morning conference, lunch, then on with the racing overalls.

If you haven't tried it you should its great fun and very competitive.

An instructor gives a safety lecture, explains the rules, and then takes you around the track in a BMW 3 series or something similar. Around the side of the track are different coloured cones to help you brake and accelerate then after a few laps instruction it's your turn. As long as you're not a complete imbecile you are then passed to take a single seater open topped whizzer around. You think you are doing a ton, maybe you are.

At Brands, as you boast with the others how fast and smooth you drove, a tall quiet man takes you by the hand and straps you into a two seater Le Mans type car and hits the throttle. 'What do you think' he shouted when we had completed our first lap, 'I thought you had to brake for corners' I replied, eyes tight shut.

'Let's go a little faster' he laughed, hit the turbo and I touched cloth. As far as I'm concerned the bends at Brands Hatch should be called, fuck it we're going too fast corner, I want my Mummy chicane, have you any toilet paper bottom bend and thank fuck for the finishing line.

Whether we got any additional business from these days I would say yes, in hindsight now I'm so far away, who cares, I enjoyed them.

Our marketing department was staffed by several prats who had no touch with reality. Perhaps I'm being a tad tough, some were from a nearer constellation than Planet Zog and some were good guys. They were always coming up with hair brained schemes to sell more power tools. Who will ever forget Rick trying to sell in a snowflake promotion to dealers in Brixton or a rotary hammer promotion that involved sending house bricks by post.

One I did enjoy was linked with miniatures of

Scotch whisky, surprising how many went astray, hic.

I missed out on the exotic distributor trips, Barbados and Rio de Janeiro, I think the boss caught a dose there, I wonder how he claimed for hookers on his expenses sheet?

I was picked for the Cyprus trip along with Peter the national sales manager, Tony Payne, Clive Boughton, Peter Halley, Sheree Dubock the new publicity manager and some other field guys.

Peter Kelly a Bob Hoskins look alike was a great boss a genuine man who didn't care how you got the business as long as it came in. Many were the afternoons I stopped off at his cottage in Dummer to have tea with him and Shirley his wife on their lawn. Somehow life at Bosch was better after a heart to heart with Peter. A tremendous amount of the success of Bosch was down to Peter's matter of fact, no bullshit, this is how it really is approach to both customers and his own team.

Sheree took over from JR head of PR a lovely man you couldn't help liking despite the cock-ups and delays in most things he touched. He organised exhibitions, the stands and tools, lighting and chairs. There were always last minute hiccups, which involved us scrabbling around to sort out by the skin of our teeth, by which time he would amble up, pint in hand and a smile on his face.

Sheree was a different cup of tea immensely talented, organised and a great figure to boot.

Hirex her first exhibition was where she and I fell out, I couldn't believe everything was going to plan so stuck my nose in. Having it smacked by Sheree I withdrew to a safe distance and watched amazed as the stand, lighting, carpet and tools all appeared and the stand looked great.

So off we flew to Cyprus with a hundred Bosch

dealers and their wives for a week's holiday. Sheree organised the whole thing, the hotel, trips, dinners even a sports day and it all ran like clockwork.

I couldn't understand why my room was so far away from everyone else until one of my pals Russell from Portatools who was also a friend of Sheree's confided in me. Sheree had heard of my reputation and wanted me as far away as possible, 'suits me' I said.

All the Bosch guys had brought their wives which left me by myself, still there were plenty of dealers who sent their wives to bed early so they could drink with their friends and 'Billy no mates Robin'!

After a few days Sheree began to thaw. We ran a sports day, nothing too strenuous, an egg and spoon race, pedalo regatta and three legged races, everyone joined in and had a great day, organised by Sheree of course.

Tony Payne was the turning mark for the pedalo race, standing up to his waist in water with a pint in his hand laughing as the dealers aimed at him.

Tony died of cancer a few years later, I saw him in hospital, a small wasted figure, so sad. At his funeral I thought of him standing in the water a smile on his face, and that's the way I will always remember Tony.

One night I got the Bosch team to perform an old act I did on the passenger ships which brought the house down. It was entitled 'If I was not employed by Bosch what would I rather be', how true those words would come to pass in the fullness of time.Sheree invited me back to her room for a nightcap. I went back to my room and filled a carrier bag with bottles and clinked my way back along the empty corridors. How often my life has gone this route, bottles and girls.

Sheree opened her door and welcomed me in. As she shut the door behind me I little realised it was the closing of a chapter and the opening of a new book.

Making Fast

As I sit here in the cockpit of my faithful friend Wizzo, the half moon behind me lighting our way forward, we are surfing along at eight knots with the Azores just a few hundred miles away, I realise how lucky I am.

These last few weeks have given me the chance to pick up my pen again and finish what I started in November 1999. Much water has passed under my keel in that time, relationships forged, old ones blurred and many a new sailing friend made. I am sadder maybe stronger for all that I have tried to achieve. Seven times across the Atlantic, twenty seven thousand sea miles give you a lot of thinking time. Time to evaluate what's right, what's wrong and what was fun. I have always worked to live not lived to work.

If you have stayed the course and reached these words then congratulations. I hope you have enjoyed my meanderings, jumbled and chaotic that they are, it is how I would like to remember my half-century on the high seas of life.

Robin Tickner

Yacht Wizzo
Lat   35.32.01 North
Long 35.59.93 West

Ps
And as Jethro would say, who's nicked my shit house roof?

Finished with Engines

I started this book as a reminiscence of my childhood, to make sure none of our family ever had an excuse not to remember our upbringing in the sixties and seventies. I'm not sure what I ended up writing but you've read it so you can form your own opinion. Whatever it is it certainly isn't art.

What I have to do is thank all the players in the book but particularly the stars, my family.

Mom and Dad, incorrigible, indestructible, indescribable and lately irresponsible, where would I be without them. To Jeremy down in Aussie with Loz his ever patient and irrepressible partner not forgetting his daughter Katie who is a young woman now. All through the recent years when my life has gone off the rails or I found my vocation depends how you read it, Jeremy has been there, encouraging and supporting. Joff with his unique sense of humour which make family gatherings even more chaotic and his wife Sandy with the well screwed on Northern head and their talented son Ben, I still owe them a tent. I can't explain now you'll have to read the next book.

But a special big and ongoing thank you must go to Buster my kid brother and to Mandi his wife. These two guys have been my financial advisors, bankers, mail forwarders, advice line, love councillors and best friends, without their e mails all over the world I could not have achieved my aims. On my last trip home from the Caribbean to celebrate my fiftieth birthday I was dumped so poor old Buster had to put up with his rufty tufty sailor brother crying as he ironed his party shirt. Not embarrassed at all he gave me a hug, my forty five year old little brother comforting his big bruv, that's what family are for. I also am the very proud uncle of their immensely talented and beautiful daughters

Maisie and Alice, I know all uncles say that but when they burst onto the UK scene you will understand. Just recently I hit another low time and was helped immensely by Andrew another old friend of the family, thanks mate.

And finally to say goodbye to Richard, the last year of his life was very difficult for all who loved him. I shall always remember our early times together and his ultimate victory over cancer by crossing the Atlantic in his own sailboat.

Richard Oxley played a huge part in my life, I miss him, fair winds my old friend and a peaceful final anchorage.

The Tickner brothers sailors one and all

If you enjoyed 'Dishonourable Discharge' here is the start of the next leg of my trials and tribulations!

'Keep your hands away from moving machinery and don't shit in the fire bucket' was Fat Barry's concluding comments to our daily health and safety lecture or 'Tool Box' as it's known down under. Donning our safety helmets and life jackets we trooped out of the site hut into the pale pre-dawn light and trudged down the sandy path to the jetty where our workboat awaited us. Swinging on board 'Kiwi Wayne' took the helm while 'Jimmy the Knife', me, Jerry my bruv and 'Veggie Bill' held tight as the boat cut a swathe through the still waters of Botany Bay. In the distance, lights of the dredgers and spreaders flickered as we prepared ourselves for another fourteen hour shift on the Sydney Desalination project or cockup as it was better known.

I'm getting ahead of myself, when we last spoke from the pages of 'Dishonourable Discharge' I was closing the door of a hotel bedroom in Cyprus.

www.ingramcontent.com/pod-product-compliance
Lightning Source LLC
Chambersburg PA
CBHW050520170426
43201CB00013B/2026